Life Skills for Teens

A Fun and Easy Guide to Develop Good Habits

(Insightful Skills That Schools Don't Teach for a Life of Happiness)

Nicholas Allen

Published By **Chris David**

Nicholas Allen

All Rights Reserved

Life Skills for Teens: A Fun and Easy Guide to Develop Good Habits (Insightful Skills That Schools Don't Teach for a Life of Happiness)

ISBN 978-1-7775324-3-7

No part of this guidebook shall be reproduced in any form without permission in writing from the publisher except in the case of brief quotations embodied in critical articles or reviews.

Legal & Disclaimer

The information contained in this book is not designed to replace or take the place of any form of medicine or professional medical advice. The information in this book has been provided for educational & entertainment purposes only.

The information contained in this book has been compiled from sources deemed reliable, and it is accurate to the best of the Author's knowledge; however, the Author cannot guarantee its accuracy and validity and cannot be held liable for any errors or omissions. Changes are periodically made to this book. You must consult your doctor or get professional medical advice before using any of the suggested remedies, techniques, or information in this book.

Upon using the information contained in this book, you agree to hold harmless the Author from and against any damages, costs, and expenses, including any legal fees potentially resulting from the application of any of the information provided by this guide. This disclaimer applies to any damages or injury caused by the use and application, whether directly or indirectly, of any advice or information presented, whether for breach of contract, tort, negligence, personal injury, criminal intent, or under any other cause of action.

You agree to accept all risks of using the information presented inside this book. You need to consult a professional medical practitioner in order to ensure you are both able and healthy enough to participate in this program.

Table Of Contents

Chapter 1: What Is Mental Hearing? 1

Chapter 2: Positive Affirmations 23

Chapter 3: Test A Patch With The Foundation 44

Chapter 4: Emotional Changes 60

Chapter 5: Supplements 83

Chapter 6: Conflicting Disagreements About Relationships 102

Chapter 7: Finding The Perfect First Home 111

Chapter 8: What Should I Bring? 132

Chapter 9: Cleaning Supplies 146

Chapter 10: Settings Of Your Washer ... 168

Chapter 1: What Is Mental Hearing?

The health of your mind can affect through your whole existence! This can impact the way you conduct yourself, manage emotions, relationships as well as your physical well-being.

Mental health refers to how you feel, think, and communicate your feelings. The state of your mental health is the mood. It's the way you feel and respond when you experience certain events occur to you.

Do you know why people begin to feel cold and suffer headaches if they're in the process of falling ill? This is a sign of a person's health. Health and mental well-being, on other hand, refers to how people feel, think, and behave, particularly when they are in stressful situations.

Maintaining your mental health maintained allows you to live your every moment to the fullest, and be able to find balance in various things. Women with good mental health may live a happy life as they manage rejection with grace, and establish healthy connections with their family and friends.

Like your physical health may be affected by a variety of microbes Your mental health may suffer when you are experiencing specific issues. My experience was the stress of school. If you're like me, it may be a family crisis as well as childhood trauma or a medical condition.

You're your mental health! If your mind is in good health and you're in good health, it's healthy for you too. Mental health is crucial since it determines every decision that you take. You can handle challenging times if you are concerned about your mental wellbeing. Also, you'll become more imaginative and open to new experiences.

Positive people attract positive people. This is why a woman with great mental health can be more successful when it comes to relationships with the people close to her. Also, she'll think clearer and be efficient, achieving the objectives she has set rapidly. She'll feel confident and comfortable about herself and enjoy a great self-esteem.

Be confident if you feel your mood doesn't look great. There are methods to make you feel more confident in your self-esteem and manage the negative thoughts. One way to boost the quality of your life is to try Cognitive Behavioral Therapy (CBT). It's an enjoyable and simple method to deal with harmful thinking habits.

What is COGNITIVE BEHAVIORAL THERMAPY?

Sometimes you feel down due to your focus on negative aspects of life. Then you forget that circumstances are good for you. CBT therapy allows your brain to forget about negative events. It helps reduce symptoms caused by various mental illnesses by redirecting your brain to focus on positive thoughts.

In the case of fail an exam You might begin thinking about whether you'll have revise the test or retake the class. The practice of CBT can help you concentrate on the way that failing the test can help you be better prepared when taking it over again.

CBT is designed to help train your brain to modify thoughts and behaviours that are negative. CBT assists you in controlling your mood and develop ways of coping to overcome issues.

CBT involves talking! The client will discuss with the therapy therapist why your feelings are the way they are, and they'll offer suggestions for better ways to manage the stress. The therapist can help you identify solutions for your mental health issues you may have been experiencing.

CORRECTING With A STRESS

Did you ever feel tired from a long day of school, and you just you wanted to curl up in bed to sleep the rest your day? The feeling you feel is known as stress.

When you are stressed, it's because you're exhausted after doing too much work or in stressful conditions for a long time. This is how your body reacts to situations which require focus.

The symptoms of stress differ for each individual. When I'm stressed out, I can be angry in a flash I lose weight rapidly as well as lose interest in the things I enjoy. The same thing happens to my siblings and may be different for your case. If you're feeling stressed, you could feel exhausted or agitated. It is also possible to suffer from frequent headaches, and experience difficulty working.

Everyone is at risk of stress There is no need to feel anxious. It's all about the response to anxiety. Do you take a step back and try to find ways to unwind? Do you get angry at your peers?

There are proven ways to reduce stress for example:

Reading

The reading experience isn't dull! It's a fantastic method to concentrate your thoughts and let it go to other things which make you stressed or stressed. Between school work as well as home chores and various other obligations, you may be unable to fall into a deep sleep. The reading of books can ease anxiety and keep you at peace.

Exercises to breathe

It's a much more peaceful way to relax than letting your breath flow slow and taking in the present. What's more, you can perform it at any time such as on the bus or in the bedroom or even in your bathroom. It is possible to do it when lying on a sofa or in bed, or even sitting in the chair.

Relax your eyes take a deep breath through your nostrils. Concentrate on each breath that you take, and how it is feeling. And then, slowly exhale with your mouth. It is possible to repeat the exercise however many times you wish. It will allow you to focus only on what's happening in the moment. This will also allow you to take a step back and make more informed choices.

Exercises for physical fitness

Stress can be relieved through physical exercise such as swimming, walking, athletics, running around the neighbourhood or doing household chores.

The physical activity can increase your confidence as well as fill you with happy hormones, also known as endorphins. This can also help keep your mind off of the things that make you anxious.

Playing music

As the disease spread, a few health centers or organizations set regular music therapy sessions with teens using videoconferencing systems. These sessions helped teens manage their emotional states by using music as a tool to help to navigate the tsunami of their emotions.

It is possible to listen to music that soothes you, like hip-hop and classical tunes. Music can stimulate your body, and gives you positivity. Thus, you can play your most loved music, sit at the mirror and be a little more fun! It's possible to imagine yourself as one of the Beyonce dancers.

Journaling

If you're not feeling like speaking to anyone about what you're feeling or are feeling, discuss your feelings with yourself by writing your feelings in a diary or journal. This will serve as a confidant and will become an excellent "listener" on the things you're afraid to share with anyone else.

Make time to write down your thoughts every day. It will allow you to be at ease with your thoughts and help you make better choices too.

Speak to someone.

Speak to someone you trust about the things that cause you stress can assist you in managing stress more effectively and develop effective solutions. This will help you gain a an entirely different perspective of the issues you're feeling and ease the weight off your shoulders.

If the cause of your anxiety is caused by a family conflict it is possible that you will feel more comfortable talking about the situation with the school counselor. If the issue is one which you're experiencing in school, make sure you speak to your parents, a older sibling or school counselor.

Practice mindfulness

The method works through focusing your entire attention on the sensations you're experiencing right now. It allows you to focus on your feelings and figure out ways to manage it.

Mindfulness training can alleviate symptoms from other ailments such as depression, anxiety, sleeplessness and even discomfort.

Be patient and absorb the world surrounding your. Use your senses to experience the senses of touch, sight, smell and the taste. Take a moment to take the time to look around take in the smell of flowers and feel the sun's rays upon your skin as you head to the park.

Maintain your open mind and focus your attention on your actions. Eliminate any idea that isn't relevant at the moment, and pay full attention to what you're doing. Enjoy it and discover happiness within the moment. Like breathing exercises, you are able to practice mindfulness anywhere and at any time.

Be yourself

In a time that is constantly changing standards and standards are constantly changing, it can feel as if that you're not getting some thing. It's possible that you feel you're supposed to improve. This is a lie!

Believing in yourself as you truly are and what you value is the best method to get rid of these emotions. Take care of your self! Make an effort to become more of a person. But don't make changes to be a part of the crowd.

Meditation

The best method to meditate is to ease tension. This means that you are calm and paying attention to yourself as well as the place where your mind is wandering. You can meditate in different ways;

1. Meditation on the body scan: Lying on your back, spread your legs and then place the arms to your sides with your palms up. Concentrate on each part of your body in a slow manner, moving from head to toe. Take note of each sensation within every part of your body.

2. Sit in a straight position with your feet laid flat on the floor, and put your hands rest on your lap. Take a deep breath through your nose and pay attention to your breaths. If you find yourself distracted or interrupted, you can take note of what the experience was as and then return to your meditation.

3. Walking meditation: Choose the quietest spot in your area and begin slow walking. Concentrate on the spot and remain alert to the feelings. Once you have reached the point where you've reached make a turn and keep moving, focusing on the sensations you feel.

ASKING for help

It's impossible to live life by yourself! It is important to have people around you. In times of crisis seeking help from other people is fine. It's easy to ask for help however it can be hard for those who've been through difficult circumstances on their own.

Perhaps you were brought up with beliefs that make difficult to seek assistance. Perhaps you've been taught that you should not;

Helping someone else could be an indication of vulnerability.

Helping others shows that you're confident and not weak. It lets you know the things you require and don't hesitate to seek help.

Instead of sayIng "I don't want my teacher and friends to know I don't understand this subject, so I will keep on trying it on my own till I get it," you can say "I will approach some of my friends that seem to understand this subject and ask them to help me."

You don't deserve help or support.

Everyone needs help! Nobody can accomplish everything independently. Therefore, it is recommended to reach out to get help. This can help improve your relationship with others. In other words rather than saying "Don't worry, I will handle this myself," add, "I appreciate your show of appreciation. I would appreciate it for you to help me".

Make sure you are cautious when approaching seeking assistance. It is best to discuss your issues with a person who is concerned and listens, not one who criticize, judge or even blame your.

There are times when you know what someone's reaction will be in certain situations, but on the rare occasion there are times when you'll be taken out of the blue and rejected. Don't fret, this isn't because of something that you've done. The issue is with someone else.

Having a Support System

There is an aid system in times whenever things don't go smoothly. People who are available to hold your hand or cheer you up and motivate you to persevere can be your support networks.

A solid support system is there to support you. They won't talk about your shortcomings. They also only motivate them to perform the proper actions.

Your family members could include the parents of your children or brother, sister, classmates, or neighbors. If you do not have a family or friends Consider participating in activities that let you meet new individuals. These are usually offered through books clubs, part-time positions or volunteering opportunities.

Although having a system of support is great, it's important to be aware that they're human too. There are times when they're in difficult times and moods and you should not overburden them with all your worries.

INTERFERING EMOTIONS WITH NEGATIVE EMOTIONS

When you are a teenager is a time when you'll encounter situations that can leave you feeling unhappy. It is possible to lose a few dollars or get into a dispute with your friend you love These kinds of situations will happen and can make you feel miserable.

Being able to handle those negative feelings come over your life is crucial. You should be aware that being unhappy does not mean an end to your existence. Feelings are a thing that can be temporary. Three steps that you can follow to deal with the negative emotions you experience:

Identify the feelings

The initial step for dealing with emotional turmoil is to recognize their presence and acknowledging the negative emotions. Alongside your emotions be aware of the way your body is feeling.

There could be sensations throughout the body. For instance, your face becomes hot, or you experience headaches in a specific area that your head is on, are experiencing tight muscles.

After you've identified the emotions, try not to put yourself in the position of blame. Instead, look into what you are feeling like you do and accept the emotions you feel as natural and normal.

Get involved

Once you have identified your feelings Please don't go away in the same manner; instead, make a change to better your situation.

Talk to somebody, get support to manage your mood or even start exercising to keep your thoughts off of what is making your sad.

Get help

There are times when, regardless of whatever you do there's a chance that you'll be unable to get rid of the negative feelings. There are times when you feel like screaming and crying throughout the day. The best approach to manage the situation is to seek assistance. Speak to a school counselor or a parent, an adult you trust or therapist will assist you in understanding your emotions more clearly and get you through the difficult situation you may be stuck in.

THE IMPACTS OF SOCIAL MEDIA

Aren't you amazed that you are able to stay in your home and connect with acquaintances across the world using your laptop or phone? The advent of social media enabled that!

Social media was developed for an important purpose: to enable people around the world to give and obtain details. But, it is extremely risky. While social media can bring benefits however, there are many negatives.

If you're on your smartphone throughout the day, talking and scrolling away. Attention to other things that are happening around you will decrease as you become dissatisfied. The excessive use of social media may cause you sleepy, feel harassed online, or be in a bind by family and friends.

And, not only that, being focused on social media can make people less productive as it takes you longer to accomplish your other tasks. If you are constantly connected to your smartphone, be sure that you don't just chat all throughout the day. Make sure you are learning new languages, cultures as well as online skills.

PROGRESSING SELF-ESTEEM

Self-esteem can be described as a feeling of joy and confidence within your self. Women with high self-esteem display confidence, self-confidence, and acceptance of the things they do. They are confident that they are worthy of their achievements. Women who have low self-esteem have a negative view of themselves. They have a hard time accepting themselves and believe they aren't sufficient.

How do you build self-esteem?

Your self-esteem developed as a young person. People in your life determine how you perceive you. If they concentrated on what they liked within you, you'd be content with your self. If they showed patience when your mistakes were made and you learned to forgive yourself and rectify the mistakes you made with patience.

But, if you're frequently scolded, bullied or bullied and scolded, you'd lose confidence in yourself. The words you use to describe yourself are a part of your memory and rapidly become element of the way you see your self.

If you think such as "I'm such a loser" or "I will never be as beautiful as the other girls," it can hurt confidence in yourself. Instead, you can say "I didn't win this time- but; maybe I will win next time," or "I'm beautiful in my way, and the other girls are beautiful in their way." The voice you speak in is comforting and can help you to accept your self more.

The voice that is in our minds is inspired by what other people have made to us but sometimes, it's our own self-pity. Therefore, in order to boost confidence in yourself, be around those that treat you with respect and express positive thoughts about yourself.

Examine your voice and yourself. within your head. Are you able to tell if it is too hard? Do you want to talk with a person like this?

Another way to boost confidence in yourself is to establish objectives and strive towards these goals, concentrate on the positive aspects of your life and then accept the flaws and shortcomings you have.

Chapter 2: Positive Affirmations

Teenage girls should keep their spirits up! Reminding yourself to be positive daily will boost your confidence and the confidence to continue on your journey.

The words of affirmation are thought-out and carefully created words that have a purposeful message for those who are listening and uttering them. Below are some instances of affirmations that you could use to affirm yourself:

1. I am sufficient; I don't need any change to get enough.

2. I'm smart, intelligent and eager to learn.

3. I'm secure and am loved by my family and friends and all those who know me.

4. My importance is paramount and my presence is crucial to me and to others.

5. I am accepting myself as I am and accept my imperfections as they define me. I am.

Hydrogen

the life of a teenage girl is full of numerous things to do. It is a time to go to the school, have a social with your classmates, participate in games, attend events, and more. These activities can expose you to the germs that can lead to illness.

We can, thankfully, eliminate the germs that cause illness and lead an active and healthy lifestyle. You need to take good care of yourself in order to make sure that these bacteria don't create sickness.

As a child My mom was the one who taught me the fundamentals of healthy hygiene. I was taught to take care of my hair, take showers frequently and floss my teeth each morning and in the evening. These were the basic things to do. There's more that proper hygiene is something nobody will talk to you about.

What is the best way to handle hygienic issues?

Good hygiene goes beyond washing your teeth or showering. Also, it involves keeping your body as well as your environment spotless.

The process isn't as complicated as it may sound. A good hygiene routine is as simple as washing your body each throughout the day by washing your hands properly when you go to the bathroom and making sure you brush your teeth at least two times a day, sniffing your nose or throwing up in a tissue and many more.

The way you treat yourself can differ based upon your cultural background and the place you reside. In certain cultures, people are required to bathe twice per day In some societies there's a requirement to shower at least twice per daily. Find out what the culture you're in expects from you, and follow this.

The teenage teens are a great opportunity to study and master the basics of hygiene.

As you get older you will find them helpful for you.

Build a healthy ROUTINEA regimen of hygiene is a routine you adhere to each day to clean your body, and clear it of bacteria. This is a great means of training yourself to be clean and well. Here's an example for what is a good hygiene practice is as:

I wash my body daily

I clean my teeth two times every day

I clean my hair frequently

I wash my hair each morning

I floss daily

I change my underwear daily

I do not wear clean clothes

I caress my fingers and toenails

I make sure to use my products for hygiene regularly e.g. the feminine and deodorant

I wash filthy clothes frequently

My hands are washed after handling animals.

Making use of the correct products for HYGIENE

The different products for hygiene can help make sure you stay clean and healthy. These include:

Deodorants: When you perform your day-to-day routine, your arms may become sweaty and create unpleasant smells. Deodorants can help fight off those unpleasant odors. Deodorants can come as sprays or in roll-on type. If the product is a spray you may use it to share with other people. But if you're using a roll-on product, it's your personal item that isn't meant to be shared.

Brush and toothpaste They are utilized to ensure that your teeth are clean. It is recommended to apply a small amount of toothpaste onto the brush, and then brush your teeth each morning and at night. Make sure you don't divulge this information to anyone.

Soaps soaps are substances that have a foamy texture which are utilized to clean. They are utilized to wash clothing, surfaces and even your own body. They eliminate germs and clean off dirt. They can come in bar or powder form, as well as cream or even liquid.

Make-up products: They can be used to enhance the look of your body or face. It includes nail polishes and lipsticks, as well as brushes as well as eye-liners, facial creams as well as other products. These products are intended for use by individuals because they're in constant contact with skin.

Shampoos are specially formulated soaps to clean your hair. They help break down the dirt that is in your hair.

Hair Care

Each girl's hair style is unique and beautiful each in its own unique way regardless of whether it's straight, curly or curly. Hair makes you appear stunning, which is why you need to maintain it.

The hair care process is all you can do to ensure your hair is good and healthy. There are a myriad of methods to maintain your hair. This can be accomplished by regularly washing your hair by oiling and conditioning it cutting the ends every so often as well as styling it with style.

Shampooing your hair regularly is beneficial for the scalp. It aids in the removal of sweat and oil from the hair's pores. A healthy and regular regimen for your hair can help to fight off dirt, excess oil, and other hair products that leave behind remnants. The scalp will be refreshed!

A healthy scalp is vital to hair growth. It is possible to wonder how massage your scalp when you clean it can increase the flow of blood to the hair. It helps grow your hair quickly. Cleaning dirt from your scalp can clear the pores. This allows hair to grow quicker.

How do you know your hair's style and the texture

There are a variety of methods to deal with the different types of hair. Therefore, you should know the hair's texture and type in order to properly treat your hair.

This guide will assist you to identify your hair's type and texture

Straight Hair

Straight hair is when the hair you have isn't straight or curly from the scalp all the way to your ends. The texture of hair is smooth and silky. There are three variations:

Your hair type: How it looks:

Curly hair

The difference is an important distinction between straight and curly hair. It's not curly, but it's also not straight. It's wavy hair when you've got a small curly pattern on your hair's ends. There are three types of this type of hair:

THE TYPE OF YOUR HAIR: HOW it looks:

Curly hair

Take a look at your hair's tips and check if there is the 'S' shape. It's the curly hair style. Curly hair could become easily knotted and you should handle it with care. There are three types of curly hair

THE TYPE OF YOUR HAIR: HOW it looks:

Coily Hair

If your hair is arranged in a "Z" shape and is curly, then it's. There is a possibility that your hair is easily broken or appears rough and rough when it's not properly maintained. The curls can be compact too. There are three types of hair that are coily:

THE TYPE OF YOUR HAIR: HOW it looks:

How do you straighten your hair using flat irons:

Get your hair ready

We'll be clear: neither shampoo or conditioner can guarantee the appearance of straight hair. Hair care products with the label "smoothing" may help prepare hair strands to be able to go through the process, by providing a significant amount of moisture.

After you have washed your hair, utilize a towel for removing any excess moisture, but make certain that your hair remains wet.

Use a heat protector

The spray is lightly applied to your hair. Avoid your scalp. After that, you can gently massage your hair wet using an untangling brush to get rid of the hair tangles.

Do some practice rough drying

Drying rough means removing the excessive moisture from hair by using a blow dryer or your fingers prior to using brushes or other hairstyling equipment. When you're done ensure that your hair is totally dry.

Beware of brushes that aren't the right ones

Make sure you put the correct brush after drying. Large tooth combs work great for extremely curly or coily hair. They will make combing the hair easy.

Avoid extreme heat

Hair types that differ require different temperatures for the flat iron. The ideal temperature is the range of 375 to 400 degrees. The temperature shouldn't surpass 450°F.

Section your hair

If you wish for your flat iron melt your hair's texture, make sure you do not straighten your hair without dividing it into sections. This can help to avoid using excessive temperatures. Carefully cut your hair so that you conserve both energy and time.

Apply Finishing Products

These products give your hair shine and keep it from frizz. It is possible to use a high-quality hair conditioner to achieve this. After applying the serum brush your hair with a comb to distribute the serum.

How to straighten your hair using an air-dryer

Get your hair ready

Rinse hair gently, wipe hair and then squeeze dry using a towel until your hair is dry. It is recommended to apply the heat protector to stop damage to your hair.

Section your hair

Hair should be divided into four sections with the comb. You should create a portion that runs from the forward to back. Make a separate part the ear to the ear. Make two pieces of the side and then pin them together. Do not do anything to the hair in the back.

Ensure that your hair is not dry.

Prior to styling your hair, place some water into an aerosol bottle. Spray your hair. It makes hair easy to manage and decreases breakage.

Comb your hair using an oversized toothcomb

Beginning at the roots of your hair, and then comb through the scalp and ends. Make sure your dryer is following your brush's direction. This will allow hair to breathe the warmth. This gives you an even texture.

Repeat the process

Once you've finished with your hair in the rear of your head, continue the same process on the front, until the hair is the length you desire.

MAKEUP

Makeup is a form of art. Makeup can be means to show off your individuality. You can play using colors to make you appear beautiful. Your natural beauty is just how you're, however, makeup can make your appearance sparkle. This can boost your self-confidence and creativity.

How do you create a plan to maintain well-maintained skin

There are many gorgeous women with complexions as clear as glass. You might be wondering why their skin appears clean and healthy. There are a few easy actions to ensure clean and healthy skin.

Skin care regimens can help slow the aging process as well as prevent numerous skin problems. It sounds interesting, right? Start by following these guidelines:

Make sure you treat your skin with the utmost attention

Beware of excessively harsh soaps! Strong soaps may strip away the natural oils which make your skin radiant. Choose mild cleanser which will not cause dry skin. After your shower and dry off, lightly pat your skin and leave your skin moist.

"Say YES to a nutritious diet

As you're growing, you must eat nutritious food items not only for healthy bones but also for beautiful skin too. A good diet is your best friend. The best thing to do is ensure that you consumed plenty of fruit and veggies. This will help your look prettier and more youthful. Additionally, it is important to take in plenty of water every day.

Wear sunscreen

Are you aware of any time that you were told not to be out in the sun without wearing sunscreen? It's because sunscreen is a protective layer protecting your skin from damaging UV rays from the sun.

Applying sunscreen regularly will help prevent wrinkles, fine lines and pores on your face. What's more is that it can help prevent skin cancers as well.

Be able to manage stress

Have you ever thought about how stress has the most severe effect on your face? Do you have any experience with those pimple-like marks on the faces of your acquaintances? They're known as stress breakouts. They are visible on the face when you're stressed.

If you're feeling anxious If you are feeling stressed, try taking deep breaths or meditative.

A variety of products for making-up

Do you know the names of some cosmetics? Are you aware of what they're used to serve? Certain makeup kits are packed with items you've not heard of. Therefore, I've put together an inventory of the most crucial makeup items you'll require when you're a teenager.

Primer

Imagine the product acting as Photoshop on your face. It can help cover pores that are large or blemishes as well as wrinkles. This helps make makeup appear and feel more comfortable. It's basically as applying a tint to your face prior to applying making your makeup.

Foundation

It can come either in cream, powder or in liquid form. The foundation can be applied on the neck and face for a flawless look or to make a more even skin tone. It can be used as the foundation to build the makeup style you want to create.

Concealer

Concealer differs in comparison to foundation due to its weight. It conceals spots and dark circles that appear on the skin. It is not necessary to be concerned about skin's imperfections because it assists to blend them in with the skin.

Eyeshadow Palette

It is possible to use eye shadow for giving your eyes a bit of dimensions and dimension. Also, you can use it to make your eye appear bigger in a pleasing manner. Eye shadows must be put on the eyelid, including the eyebrows.

Eyeliner

You've probably seen the Smoky eye effect of some women before. The cosmetic product that gives the look is known as Eyeliner. It is a simple product that highlights the central part of your face, and increases the eye's color.

Mascara

Do you wish your lashes to appear longer and more dense? If yes then mascara is your preferred cosmetic product. The mascara makes natural lashes appear more full and more voluminous.

Setting Powder

Setting powder can be used to make your makeup look more firmly on the skin. It can be applied by pressing or loosely shaped. It will keep your face looking perfect to the maximum extent possible. Additionally, you can use it to get rid of any excess shimmer from your face.

Bronzer

Applying to add a touch of the appearance of warmth. They are designed to give your skin a radiant glow. They are also available in powder, gel cream or in liquid in liquid.

Lipstick

Lipsticks provide texture and colour to the lips. One of the best things about lipsticks is that they come in several different color variations. It is possible to pick your favorite shade or one that you are most comfortable wearing.

Discovering The Perfect Product For Your Skin Tone

Applying products to your face which do not complement the color of your face can result in an absolute nightmare. We wouldn't want you to put in the cash, time and energy only to appear as clowns.

At the time I was around your age I was not aware of which makeup products to use that matched my skin tone. I picked products that were lighter shades than my complexion which looked weird.

Make sure you choose items that complement your skin's tone. If not, then your makeup could fail.

Know your skin shade

Every person has their own tone! Therefore, you must first determine your type of skin. Are you tan, dark, or fair? There's a few things to consider Different makeup brands may recognize skin tones using different numerals or names. Choose your color and stay to the color.

Identify your undertone

The hue of your undertone is beneath your skin, which affects the overall color of your skin. For you to choose the most suitable makeup products to suit your skin, it is important first understand what the word "undertone" signifies. For determining your undertone take note of the veins that appear on the wrist. If you're cool-toned your veins may appear either purple or blue, however If you're warmer-toned the veins will be to be green.

Chapter 3: Test A Patch With The Foundation

Once you've identified the skin tone and shade and undertone, it is time to test various foundation shades. The best way to test is to apply a small amount of foundation onto your jawline in order to determine the ideal shade for your foundation. It is a good idea since your jawline doesn't exhibit the redness different areas of your face might be displaying. This can help you determine the right color for your foundation.

Buy foundation and concealer from the same range

When you have identified the skin tone you have and are aware of what foundation you like perfectly, it's easy to identify the concealer that can also be a good shade. The easiest way is to get both of the same brand.

How do you properly take care of complexion tone and color

As time passes, neglecting your skin can cause acne and changes in color and appearance. In order to avoid problems like this You should

Boost your water content

Whichever shade of skin you have the need for a balanced amount of moisturizing every day. If you're a dark-skinned person specifically, your skin may be dry fast. Make sure to add an eye moisturizer to your routine. It's not like the lotion for your body or that you are using on a daily basis.

Be careful when handling sensitive skin.

If your face is sensitive to things quickly, you may have sensitive skin. Skin becomes dry and red.

Make sure you are aware of the products you put on your skin. Look for products with the words "sensitive skin" or "fragrance-free."

Beware of sun damage to your skin

Exposure to sunlight for a long time could cause your skin to respond negatively. If you are spending the majority of your time in sunlight, use sunscreen that has the highest SPF, which is around 30-50.

What should you do to properly take care of your skin after taking off makeup?

This is what you need to apply to your skin following taking off your makeup:

Steam your face just prior to washing your face.

Apply your face to an ice-cold bowl of hot steaming water for about a minute and then watch it work it's magic. The pores begin to appear more open and the cleanser will be absorbed deep into the skin.

Do not scrub your face.

Cleansing your face after you have removed your makeup creates small tears to appear on your skin. It's awful, isn't it? The stinging motions can cause irritation to the skin, making it appear red. The best method is to use fingertips.

Nourish your skin

It's best to apply a toner serum, or moisturizer right after you take off the makeup. A toner can restore the correct pH balance to your skin. Additionally, it will remove the make-up that your cleanser might not have removed.

Serums are brimming with antioxidants and vitamins to nourish your skin. It is also recommended to apply a moisturizer in order to maintain the moisture of your skin.

SAVING

Hair grows on girls' armpits and around their pubic area when they reach puberty. This can cause discomfort or hold germs that cause unpleasant odors if you do not get rid of them. If you're seeing the growth of hair in these regions, you could be wondering about the best way to cut it off. These are the things to think about to ensure the perfect shaving experience

Do not cut your hair dry.

The dry shaving process can result in irritation and burns to the skin, making your skin dry and unpleasant. The best way to treat your skin is to soak approximately 10 minutes with warm water in order to ease the surface of skin. In addition, exfoliating products can to prepare the skin to be shaved.

Make sure to use cool water

It is possible that you are a lover of showering in very hot water. However, prior to shaving, make sure to reduce the temperature a bit. If the water you are bathing in is excessively hot, it could cause your skin to become extremely fragile and susceptible to cuts.

Use shaving cream

Avoid using soap instead of shaving cream. As with many women who think that soap and water work as fluids to smooth skin. But it could dry your skin.

Shaving foam or gel acts as a oil to the skin. This will assist keep your skin moist after shaving.

Wash thoroughly

Once you've done shaving, you can use cool water to flush off the foam. This can help to close your pores. Then application, you should apply a hydrating moisturizing cream or self-tanning cream to keep your skin from drying out.

FEMAINE Medical Appointments

If your body is experiencing modifications, it is important to make plans for visits or meetings with medical experts to assist your. In this book, I'll provide some basic information within this guide, however it is still necessary to consult doctors to offer guidelines for your specific physical and age. It is possible to begin seeing health professionals from 12 to 15 years old.

What can you expect from your trip

Be calm! Your initial visit with your doctor is focused in getting to know the doctor you see and talking about your medical past. There may be a need to take a physical. It will check your blood pressure, sugar level levels, the weight and your height.

Your visit is likely to be both interactive and informative. The doctor may discuss innovative ways of maintaining good health.

The frequency of appointments

It is important to note that the frequency and duration of female appointment will depend on the health of your entire. In general, you will only have to visit your physician at least once per year. If you have unusual or painful menstrual cycle or vaginal discharge that is unusual, it is possible to schedule the appointment of your physician prior to the time.

What questions should you ask you Gynecologist

It's weird asking your doctor some questions about you personally isn't it? It was me too. I was anxious and afraid. Your doctor is skilled and well-trained to address your concerns. The only thing you must do is to relax and look for the clarity you need.

Here are a few concerns you could discuss with your gynecologist.

1. My period is coming later?

2. What's that white stuff that is In my underwear?

3. What is the reason my vagina gets itchy?

4. What is the best way to conduct an exam for self-breast?

5. Are the food choices I make influence my menstrual cycle?

6. My cramps are incredibly painful. What could I do to lessen the discomfort?

HPV Vaccine

HPV means Human Papillomavirus. It causes a variety of cervical cancers, as well as cancers of the vulva oropharynx and vagina as well as the anus. There's a vaccine available that will stop the growth of HPV. This is known as HPV Vaccine. HPV Vaccine. The vaccine is also effective against HPV forms that cause various genital warts. The best time to receive this vaccine when you are in your teens to prevent becoming infected.

Skincare and sunscreen

You can take steps to ensure your skin is supple and healthy. A good example of ingredients to protect your skin is sunscreen.

Sunscreen shields your skin from damaging effects from the sun. It can help prevent sunburns, wrinkles and also reduces the risk of developing cancer.

It's possible to be awestruck by the way sunscreen shields you greatly.

It absorbs UV radiation of the sun's (UV) radiation and prevents it from reaching different parts of your skin. It is recommended to apply sunscreen about 30 minutes prior to going out in the sun.

You should use sunblock every day

Sunscreen is a great way to prevent discoloration and dark spots. This helps to maintain a smoother, more evenly toned skin. The sunburn may also cause the production of oil and increase the severity of acne. If you apply sunscreen, you can stop the acne from becoming worse.

The best way to keep acne at bay and then treat it

As a young person I was blessed with flawless and silky skin. It's easy to imagine my anxiety in the middle of transitioning into teenagerhood and saw pimples appear across my face. I was self-conscious and even was embarrassed. This is why I tried everything to keep acne to develop on my face.

Acne is a normal occurrence for teenagers. It's a sign you're experiencing the puberty stage. I can understand how uncomfortable it feels to have acne However, there are solutions to control the issue.

Wash your face at a minimum twice per day.

Do not make your pimples bigger or rub your face with dirty fingers

Do not drink sugary beverages like soda

Make sure you drink plenty of water

Wash your face with cool water

Consult a dermatologist to get individual skin care recommendations

Activity: PERSONAL HYGIENE SHOPPING LIST and CHECKLIST

It's common to let your healthy hygiene practices slip by occasionally. If you allow items to fall far over a long period, poor routines could take over those that are good. This shopping list as well as routine checklists can be used as a guideline to ensure you maintain an organized routine.

If you're shopping make sure you check off your items on your personal list of hygiene items.

The PUBERTY

I Remember the first time that I noticed a change within my body. Hair began to grow in new locations and my voice began to soften. I was unsure of why I was experiencing this. One day, I made the decision to speak with my mom. This was my first experience when I was aware of puberty.

My mother explained to me the girl's body undergoes particular changes in puberty, in preparation for becoming an adult. She also talked to me about breast development, periods as well as other changes in the body as puberty progresses.

While I was a somewhat scared, I felt at ease knowing my situation. Additionally, I realized that everyone goes through puberty, which is normal phase of growing up. In time, I grew more at ease with my changing body, and accepted the changes.

You're likely to be uncertain of the changes that are taking place when you enter puberty. Don't fret, I've got your back! The chapter that follows I'll explain the definition of puberty and how to recognize the changes that occur from puberty and the ways you can take care of yourself during the period.

When you finish this chapter it will be clear that puberty is merely an era and you'll be an attractive, confident woman, ready to face the world. Let's get started!

What is PUBERTY?

The time of puberty is when your body begins to grow and grow. It prepares you so it is possible to be a parent. Also, it can be a rapid period of hormonal and physical changes which take place in the body when you grow as you grow from childhood to teenage.

The girls typically start puberty between the age from 8 to thirteen years of age. But, that isn't a guarantee that puberty won't occur sooner or later. At this point you will experience changes in your body due to natural substances, also known as hormones. It is important to be prepared and aware of the most effective way to handle the changes that you experience as you enter puberty. Learn to understand how your body works to take care of the health of your body and mind.

In puberty, you'll be able to notice changes in the appearance of your body (body changes) as well as your mood. The changes may differ with each woman, which means the experience you have may differ from the experience of your peers and may occur in different ways.

As you grow older, you'll become larger, your breasts grow larger and hair growth will begin to increase on certain parts on your body. Although these changes may be difficult, know that these are normal aspect of growing up.

BODY CHANGES

A prime indications of puberty is the growth of breast buds. The breast bud can be described as an insignificant bump growing under the nose. When the breast buds expand there is a possibility of feeling sensations of tingling, aching or a rash within the chest. The dark region between the nose (the areola) is likely to grow bigger. At around 11 years old Your body is able to produce excessive levels of estrogen hormone. Estrogen can cause breasts to expand. In this period your breasts can become sensitive and swollen, as well as your nipples could become more delicate. It's a normal aspect of this process and not something to worry about. It's the beginning of becoming an adult woman!

A different change that you can expect in puberty is a rise in the height. This is because of the accelerated growth that happens in this period, and could result in you becoming by several inches in only two months.

Chapter 4: Emotional Changes

Like I said earlier that puberty is thrilling and nerve-wracking for females. Alongside changes to your body it also brings psychological changes in this stage.

Do you feel overwhelmed and lost in the emotions you experience? It's difficult, but remember that you're not the only one! The ability to change your emotions is an integral element of development. There's a broad range of changes in your emotions that you may go through. We'll take a look each one at a time.

Mood changes

Do you ever feel as if that you're in a rollercoaster and not even in the theme park? The mood swings can be one of the major emotions you'll feel in the puberty stage. The changes in hormones that take place within your body may cause abrupt changes in mood or irritation. There are times when you feel content in some moments and unhappy within the next. While you may have conflicts with family members and friends, ones, you should remember that your mood swings are not yours to blame It will eventually ease off, and you'll be able to relax.

Self-esteem

It is possible that you notice a new shape in your body, and you'll find yourself feeling like you're not the same as your previous self. You may begin to compare your self to others and make the impression that you do not quite measure up to others. It can all take away your confidence in yourself.

Everyone develops in a different way and in their own way. Also, there isn't a "perfect" body type. All it depends is what you think of your self. Your worth is unique for who you are! Therefore, you should focus on becoming who you really are.

Stress and anxiety

Puberty may bring on many new social pressures as well as challenges that can lead to anxiety and stress. When you reach puberty, you begin worried about relationships, blending in and forming new acquaintances. It could cause anxiety and emotional stress especially if you don't achieve their requirements.

Excited emotions

It is possible that you feel more emotions like anger, joy and sorrow than in the past. Additionally, the emotions may be more intense than they were before. It is due to hormone changes within your body may affect the way you express and think about emotions.

Your PERIOD

One of the biggest changes that occur during puberty is menstrual onset which is also known as the "period." Menstruation is regular vaginal bleeding which occurs during a girl's monthly cycle. Each month, the body begins to prepare for pregnancy. If there is no birth the Uterus is cleansed of its lining and the tissue and blood of the uterus are ejected from your body through the vagina.

The typical age at which the girl to begin her period is 12. It can start at any age, from 8 to up to 16. This will be different for each girl. It is usually affected by genetics, diet as well as overall health.

Prior to the start of your period, you might observe other changes to your body. These include the development of pubic hairs and breast growth as well as the increasing weight. These all indicate when your period will begin.

Being aware of what's going on with the body is crucial. This way, you'll be able to control your menstrual cycle. That includes knowing the length of your period (the average lasts 28 days but could vary from 21 days to 35 days) and how you can plan to manage your period when you go to places or taking part in sports, as well as being aware of which products for women will work best for you.

Understanding how to manage the symptoms of menstrual cramps like bloating in the stomach, bloating and mood swings is crucial. The symptoms can be controlled through hot compresses making use of painkillers, establishing regular eating routines, and working out.

Another important thing to be aware of is that your menstrual cycle can indicate your general health. Unusual periods or excessive bleeding could indicate an underlying health issue. Seeing a doctor is important if issues develop.

What are the best ways to handle your menstrual cycle?

Controlling your menstrual cycle isn't easy. However, a variety of items for women and useful tips will make your experience easier.

Additionally, managing your menstrual cycle involves finding out what is the best for you. If it's pads, tampons cups for menstrual flow, or the most absorbent of underwear, pick a solution that makes you feel confident and at ease.

What feminine products are most effective?

If you are looking for products for women, there are various options that you can pick from. These include pads, menstrual cups and absorptive underwear. We'll go over each one of them.

Tampons

Tampons are compact, small and can be worn in the internal. They're a great option for those who are active and wish to keep the routine you have established. But, they must be replaced at intervals of between 4 and 8 hours in order to avoid poisonous shock symptoms.

Cups for menstrual flow

The cups for menstrual flow are worn in the internal. They are able to be worn for as long as 12 hours. They can be reused, environmentally friendly as well as cost effective for the long-term.

Menstrual pads

Menstrual pads are an excellent alternative if you want the protection of an outside. They are worn on the outside and connected to the underwear. They also come in a variety of sizes, absorbencies and forms.

Absorbent underwears

Absorbent underwears have a lot of similarities to menstrual pads, except they're integrated into the underwear. They're an ideal and discrete choice for women in a hurry.

When it comes to your clothing, it's recommended to dress in dark pants throughout your period since lighter hues can show bloodstains. It is also recommended to keep extra feminine products to help you deal with sudden fluctuations in your flow.

Which are the most effective feminine items

The size of the female product is dependent on personal preferences and must meet the specific requirements of your body during menstrual cycles. It is due to the fact that every woman's body, and her menstrual cycle are different.

Don't limit yourself! It is possible to experiment with various brands to discover what works best for your needs, and always keep a supply of different items to adapt to changes in the course of your work.

Female products are available in a variety of dimensions and forms. So, choosing the correct kind of size and shape is vital to keep your personal hygiene in check and feel comfortable during your entire cycle. Let's take a look at these items.

Pantyliners

Pantyliners are the most thin of all product. They're designed to allow light moderate to moderate discharge. They are typically in the middle or beginning of your time. These can be utilized regularly to guard against leaks and spots, or just for general freshness.

Regular Pads

Regular pads are designed for typical days on your cycle. Based on the needs of your cycle they're designed to absorb a small amount of discharge. They are also available in various lengths, widths and absorption levels. Regular pads can be utilized in lieu of Tampons when there is a lot of pressure.

Pads with heavy-duty construction

The heavy-duty pads are designed suitable for the most heavy days of your cycle where you'll have most discharge. They're more thick and absorptive than standard pads.

They can be found in longer lengths for better protection and coverage.

Extra-long pads

Extra-long pads are specifically designed to provide nighttime protection, so you can stay safe and comfortable while you sleep. They're wider and longer than normal pads and provide better coverage and protection for your clothes and bedding sheets.

What is the best method to cleanse the areas of your personal hygiene, and which products you should avoid

Cleaning your intimate areas is crucial to maintaining your the health of your body and maintaining hygiene. To prevent irritation and other irritations, it's important to pay attention to the way you wash your intimate areas and the products you utilize. Here are some suggestions about how you can clean your personal space and what products to avoid using while you're having your period.

Use gentle products

In the course of your menstrual cycle and menstrual cycle, stay clear of harsh shower gels, which can take away the skin's natural oils and lead to irritation and dryness. You should instead opt for mild, non-scented soap or an intimate cleanser with a pH balanced to ensure the pH balance of bacteria in your private part of your.

Wipe the entire front the back

After you have used the toilet Always clean your toilet between the front and back of your body in order to stop the transfer of bacteria through the anus and into the vagina. This will help lower the chance of developing UTIs.

Refresh your sanitary product regularly

When you're going through the period, it is important to wash your pads and tampons frequently to keep your intimate areas fresh and dry. Letting them sit over a long period of time can raise the chance of contracting an infection particularly if they get sweaty or uncomfortable.

If you feel an itchy, irritated or irritation You may need to test another brand of tampon, pad, or pads or speak with a doctor to determine if you have something else going on.

Wear breathable underwear

In the summer, wearing breathable clothes throughout your period lets air to circulate, and helps keep your intimate areas clean. Avoid tight-fitting clothing or other synthetic fabrics that could hold in moisture, increasing the likelihood of getting infections.

Rinse regularly

It is the primary element of your clean. Utilize warm water along with mild, non-scented soap to scrub your private area. Be sure to thoroughly rinse and then gently dry.

It is tempting to utilize a shower head to cleanse the vagina's interior however, it can alter the balance of pH in the intimate region, leading to an increase in the chance of contracting an infections. Instead, try using the shower head with a removable attachment to wash the interior of your vagina using water.

SPEAKING TO YOUR BODY

Being aware of your body's signals means being aware of the body's signals and recognizing what it requires. This is essential for you as your body's constantly shifting and evolving. When you are listening to your body's signals it will help you improve your overall health as well as maintain your both mental and physical health.

There are a few easy and practical ways to do self-care throughout your period. Take note that self-care is not an option to indulge in; it's an absolute necessity. Don't be reluctant to treat yourself well and participate in activities for self-care that rejuvenate your energy. These are a few practices that teenage women can engage in during the period.

Taking baths

Exercising

Hot tea is a hot drink.

Getting cozy

Note down the menstrual cycle

Attention to the physical sensations

Participating in stress-reducing activities such as meditation or breathing exercises

PHYSICAL HEALTH

Since my teens in my teens, I've been a fan of playing athletics and staying physically active. I'm particularly good at sports. I played for our school on the level of state and received the gold medal. It was that easy!

Prior to that I was not feeling my most efficient. I always felt tired and my clothing was less comfortable. In rehearsals, it was easy to feel so lazy. Then I realized that I was in need of an effort to change. Then, I began searching at methods to boost my overall health.

I made healthier choices in my food and started taking note of what I was eating. I made sure to include plenty of fruits veggies, healthy proteins. In addition, I quit eating fast food and started making more homemade meals.

Every day I'd go on strolls or runs. Then, before I knew it I felt better than I had ever felt! I felt more energy and felt more energized. I also was sleeping better in the evening. If you choose to make healthier decisions, you'll be good and lead a in a healthy, energetic life. Talk about healthy choices you have as teenagers.

EXERCISE

While exercising, blood circulation increases. This facilitates the faster delivery of nutrients and oxygen into the cells. This means that your muscles, joints, and bones will remain strong and flexible. You can then move without restriction and pursue the activities you want to do!

As a teenager there are numerous motives to incorporate exercise into the daily routine of your daily routine. We'll look at a few of them!

Mental and emotional health benefits Regular exercise is a great way to help to feel more relaxed both physically and mentally. While you're exercising and your body is releasing endorphins. They are a substances that naturally occur in the body and can assist to boost your mood and decrease anxiety. That's why you might be feeling a sense of satisfaction and peace following a workout.

Improved Self-Image: Self-image as well as self-esteem have become a common issue for adolescents today. There a constant desire to perform in line with other peers and allow for body-contrasts. This is detrimental to your mental and physical health.

It's possible that exercise is an escape from this! It can improve the self-image of yours and boost self-esteem. Exercise can make to improve your mood and create confidence in your appearance.

Increased energy and physical health regular exercise can help keep an ideal weight, and decrease the chance of developing cardiovascular disease and diabetes. In addition, it increases your energy levels, so you'll feel more awake and awake.

For you to begin exercising it is necessary to create plans. As an example, you could set a goal to work out for at least 20-30 mins every day, for 3 days per week. This gives your body the time needed to rest between sessions and will help you achieve steady outcomes. Consider substituting the time you spend on TV and surfing the internet to exercise.

There's no need go to the gym in order for exercise! Try a variety of simple workouts at home. From dancing, running, and walking. There's no limit to the possibilities! Pick an activity that is enjoyable for you to ensure that you stick to it for the long haul.

No matter what you choose Start slowly, and build slowly is crucial. Your body will require enough time to get used to the demands that your body is enduring. It's possible to start by doing only a couple of minutes of workout daily and increment the number of minutes when you're more at ease.

A workout partner can be a great way to make you more conscious in your training. The person you workout with is aware of where you are as well as what you're doing. They'll keep an eye on your movements.

Training is only one aspect of living a healthier way of life. For you to feel at your best it is also important to consume a healthy diet. A healthier diet means eating healthy, balanced meals of vegetables, fruits as well as grains and protein. Let's discuss the next step!

Healthy eating

Healthy eating is about eating food that is healthy for the body. It is about making the right choices in your diet which provide you with enough nutrition for you to operate at your highest everyday. From sports to school and beyond A healthy and balanced food plan can make you feel healthier, look more attractive and be better at every aspect of your life.

One of the main positives of eating healthy is that it will help to maintain your weight. The reason for this is that healthy food generally fill you up and are calorie-free. A healthy and balanced diet may aid in reducing the chance of developing certain diseases, such as heart disease, diabetes and some types of cancer.

Consuming a balanced diet vital for living a healthy life. An enlightened diet is one that includes various kinds of foods in a proper amount to obtain the essential nutrients the body requires. An appropriate diet must include these elements:

Vegetables and fruit They're not boring! They're an excellent source of minerals, vitamins as well as fiber. The vegetables can be prepared with a variety of ways to enhance their taste. They can be cooked with olive oil, and then add your preferred spice blend, sauté them in some sauce or even eat raw, with dips or spreads.

The same way fruit makes a wonderful snack or dessert. Cut up a piece of fresh fruits and serve them with ice cream, yogurt or even whipped cream. It is also possible to create fruit smoothies or salads.

The fruits and vegetables are great for digestion, and can improve eye, heart and overall well-being. Aiming to consume at least five servings of fresh fruits and vegetables per day is recommended.

With a little imagination it is possible to be able to get the right nutrients for a healthy lifestyle and be content. Therefore, make your vegetables and fruits the focus of your food!

Foods with starch The starchy food group is high in carbohydrates. They are a vital fuel source. Find cereals, breads and pasta that are made of all-whole grains.

Proteins: The best sources of protein are lean cuts of meat and poultry, as well as fish eggs, as well as beans and eggs.

If you're a vegetarian it is important to ensure that you are receiving sufficient protein. This can be achieved through focusing on legumes, lentils, beans, and tofu.

There are many ways to mix protein sources that are plant-based. As an example, you could mix beans with rice and rice, or make a peanut butter sandwich.

Dairy Products: Dairy dairy products are excellent sources of calcium. Calcium is crucial for solid bones. It is possible to choose dairy products with low fat items to ensure that your consumption of calories is within a reasonable range.

Fats are the most important ingredient in healthy eating, however selecting the appropriate types of fats is essential. Healthy fats that are good sources are nuts, seeds avocados, avocados, as well as olive oil.

What to eat You should limit food and beverages that contain salt, sugar and fats that are unhealthy. This is the case for carbonated and sugary drinks, chocolate as well as fried food. Instead, opt for water and tea with no sweetener or low-fat milk for your beverage. Make sure you make healthy habits that you are able to keep for the long haul.

The list of healthy foods will not be enough without water. Drinking water is crucial for the body. It regulates body temperature as well as keeps your skin moist. It is recommended to drink at least 8 cups of fluids a each day. It is possible to carry around the water bottle with you, sip glasses before or after eating drinking water in place of sweet drinks.

If you do this it will make you feel healthier as well as look and be more productive. Therefore, make healthier choices and feel the advantages of eating healthy!

Chapter 5: Supplements

The use of supplements is a fantastic method to ensure you're getting the minerals, vitamins as well as other vital elements your body needs for proper functioning. It is essential to understand that supplements to your diet aren't always a necessity. Sometimes there are risks to it.

A lot of people use supplements in order to treat a lack in one particular nutrient for example, iron and vitamin D. Iron is a crucial mineral that aids your blood to transport oxygen to the rest of your body. an absence of iron may cause anemia. Anemia can be characterised by fatigue, weakness as well as other signs. Vitamin D can, however aids in the absorption of calcium. It is vital to build strong bones as well as general good health.

If you're worried about levels of vitamin D or iron talking to your doctor prior to beginning an exercise regimen. Doctors can conduct an easy blood test to identify your deficiencies.

Like I said previously, supplementation isn't necessarily essential. Consuming a healthy diet could supply all the essential nutrients that your body requires. In particular, you could not require an iron supplement if are eating a balanced diet full of iron-rich food items like chicken, red meat and green leafy vegetables. Similar to that, if your get ample sun exposure and consume foods that are enriched with vitamin D like cereal and milk and other cereals, then you don't need an vitamin D supplement.

If you are unable to receive all the essential nutrients the body requires from food, supplements can aid in ensuring you receive everything your body needs.

Recognizing ALLERGIC REACTIONS

Being aware of food allergies can be lifesaving for everyone, particularly adolescents who are growing autonomous and are beginning to make the decisions for their own eating.

An allergy to food is the immune system's reaction when you eat a food, which is normally safe for the majority of people. It can happen within the hours or minutes following eating the food. It can also range between mild and severe. We'll look at the most common methods to recognize it below.

Skin reactions like hives, itching or swelling of lips, the face and throat.

Gastrointestinal symptoms include nausea and vomiting, abdominal pain diarrhoea.

Respiratory symptoms include sneezing, running nose, shortness or breath, wheezing or wheezing.

The symptoms of a circulatory disorder are lightheadedness and fainting, fast heartbeat or low blood pressure.

Medical attention should be sought immediately in the event that you suffer from one of these signs after eating. Be aware of what foods you're intolerant to can help you prevent food allergies So, always check the labels of your food carefully. The most frequent food allergens that cause allergic reactions are peanuts, tree nuts milk, eggs and soy. Wheat, gluten, and seafood.

If you dine at a restaurant Ask about the ingredients in your dish and let the server know about your food sensitivities. It is also possible to bring your own food items that are safe if you can't come across safe choices while eating at a restaurant.

GETTING sufficient sleep

When you are a teenager you go through various physical and mental transformations. This is why sleep is vital to assist your body cope with these changes efficiently. More than just sleep, you need adequate rest. Sleeping enough is getting into a state of relaxation where the body and your mind have enough period of time to refresh.

The average teen needs between 8 to 10 hours sleeping every at night. The ideal time for sleep is around 9-10pm. A good night's sleep boosts your ability to concentrate, memory and decreases anxiety and stress.

In the teen years when your body's rhythm shifts in a way that you find yourself more awake in night and sleepy in morning. That's why it's important to set a routine time to bed in order to are getting enough sleep.

Establish a consistent bedtime routine: It is possible to make a routine of your bedtime when you go to bed and rising each day, even during weekend. You could, for instance, schedule your bedtime at 8 p.m. and get up around 6 am the next day. This can help regulate the body's cycle of sleep and wake.

Do not drink too much caffeine. It can stimulate your brain and keep your mind alert. Therefore, staying away from drinks that contain caffeine, like tea, coffee and energy drinks. This is the best prior to going to going to bed.

Be sure to limit screen time prior to the time you get to sleep: You may have thought you were being rude to your mom in preventing you from checking your phone prior to going to going to bed. But she's a fan of you, and I'll show you the reason. Blue light emitted by the screen of your smartphone or computer may interfere with your body's production and release of melatonin an hormone that can help you get to sleep. Additionally, prolonged exposure to screens before the bedtime routine keeps your mind engaged. Therefore, you could be unable to relax. Therefore, you should avoid screen time at the very least for one hour prior to bedtime.

Make sure you have a tranquil room: Maintaining your bedroom cool, dark and calm can make it easier to sleep faster and remain asleep for longer.

Take a hot shower: Taking a warm shower before bed is a good option to rest well during the evening. It can help reduce tension in your muscles and relax your mind.

Stay active throughout your day. Regular exercise helps you to sleep better when you go to bed. It is recommended to aim for 30 minutes or more in moderate physical activity each day and that doesn't mean biking, dancing, walking as well as running.

HOW TO ACT IF YOU Are Sick

One of the most crucial things to do if you're sick is to take good care of your body. Take a lot of time off drinking fluids and consume healthy food. You can take a break from routines and activities socially to reinvigorate your body and mind to be the most beautiful version of yourself.

If you're suffering from headaches or throat soreness You can ease the pain with over-the-counter medicines. The same goes for when you're feeling nauseated it is best to avoid eating the consumption of solid food and instead stick with transparent liquids such as drink or water that contains electrolytes.

If your symptoms last longer than two days, you must see your doctor.

ADMINISTERING FIRST AIDE

The unexpected can be a nightmare! You're having a good time with a pal as you walk to the shopping mall, but one minute later, you're noticing that you're witnessing your friend bleeding from the moment she was unable to walk properly and ended up falling. That's why having an emergency kit for first aid is vital.

There are various first-aid procedures that you could learn. The specifics depend on the situation of the person being treated. If, for instance, there's bleeding, it's best to apply pressure directly on the area with the aid of a clean, dry cloth to stop bleeding. If you notice a burning then you should apply cool water over the area at least for 10 minutes to lessen the discomfort and avoid any further injuries.

Being able to take proper care of yourself when have a medical issue and mastering fundamental first aid techniques are important skills you should be equipped with.

It is possible to learn the basics of first aid techniques at schools as well as in community centers. It is important to be attentive when the topic is debated.

How to improve your self-esteem

Being a teenager and feeling assured and comfortable with the person you are can be demanding. This could be due to peer pressures and social expectations. A need to be able to identify with others, be measured up and make comparisons is a perfect recipe for lowering the self-esteem of yours. What can you do to get confidence in yourself?

Self-care is a must: taking good care of yourself is essential for building self-esteem. It is possible to exercise regularly, eat well and take enough rest. Being mindful of both your mental and physical health helps you feel assured about your skills as well as your appearance.

Be around positive individuals: Surrounding yourself with friendly and positive people will significantly boost the self-esteem of your. Inviting people to boost and inspire your development can create a comfortable and comfortable environment to build confidence.

Set goals that are achievable Set and achieve realistic goals will give you an euphoria and boost self-esteem. It's as simple as deciding to read a novel or learn new skills or even volunteer to do volunteering in your local community.

Accept compliments. Accepting compliments may be a challenge, particularly those who have low self-esteem. Yet, accepting compliments in a graceful manner and trusting them will increase confidence.

Focus on your strengths. Instead of worrying about your weak points instead, concentrate on the strengths you have and what you excel in. It will help you be more confident in yourself and in your capabilities. If it's talent in music, arts or sports, focussing on the strengths you have can help build confidence and boost self-esteem.

AFFECTIVENESS: DAILY EXERCISE TRACKER

In order to fill in the table note down the type of workout you performed every day, and the number of minutes of time you spent doing it on the "Duration (minutes)" column.

When you are done with your week, you should add up the total amount of time that you workout each day. That will give you the total amount of time did your exercise for this week.

FRIENDSHIP

Sharon is among my most cherished friend. We became friends in high school as teenagers. The girl was extremely sweet and smart. She struggled with low self-esteem, and was usually alone. She was unable to integrate as well as making new friends. This led her to feel lonely.

On a particular day, as I walked back from school I bumped into her. We spoke about schools, hobbies as well as our passions. Surprised, I discovered that she was funny of humor, and she was very welcoming. It was the beginning of what was to become an amazing relationship.

As time passed, Sharon began to open her heart to me. Sharon spoke to me about issues with self-esteem. I understood her and told her about how unique she was. I made her realize that she deserves every happiness and love all around her.

Our friendship grew and we spent our spare time laughing, talking and playing. The years passed and we all went off to various schools. But, even through that the bond remained strong. We'd talk to each on the phone or by writing correspondence. Whatever the circumstances took us our paths, we've always had our backs.

In the meantime, Sharon's transformation was astonishing. Her attitude towards life has changed from the time we were in high school. She began to see herself as positive and no longer was feeling alone. It has been her experience the importance of having support from friends and inspire your growth can make a big impact.

That's exactly what great friendships are about! Being there for each other as well as supporting one another as well as many other things.

HOW DO I CONNECT FRIENDS

The idea of making friends may seem overwhelming particularly when you're starting an entirely new institution or looking to broaden the circle of your friends. Don't be worried because it's not as difficult as you might think! Here are some helpful tips to help you meet acquaintances and be more friendly and confident.

Participate in school clubs Clubs at school provide a wonderful opportunity to connect with new people with similar interests. Whatever your passion is, whether it's arts, sports, music or any other thing you're likely to find an organization that is right to suit your needs. A club membership allows you to meet people that share similar interests. This will help build strong and long-lasting friendships.

You must be a good listener. When speaking with someone, pay the person your complete attention and be interested in the things they have to say. They will feel respected and appreciated as well as help create a stronger bond.

Be authentic You must be authentic when making new acquaintances. Be yourself and not pretend to be something who you aren't just to blend with others or impress them. Let your individuality show through and you'll be self-confident in your own persona. It will be easier for others to get in touch to you, and will appreciate the person you are.

Put yourself out in the world: Making new acquaintances involves stepping out of your comfort area. Start by initiating discussions, join clubs or even attend social events. At first, you may be nervous or shy But the more you are willing to put yourself on the table your self, the more confident will feel.

Positive: A positive outlook will make all the difference when it comes to making acquaintances. People naturally gravitate towards people who are welcoming and positive, so make sure to be positive and focus on the best aspects of life, and radiate positivity everywhere you are.

Volunteering: It's an excellent way to get acquainted with new people and do some good for the neighborhood. The group of volunteers will collaborate in order to accomplish a common objective. This will help you form solid bonds and relationships.

Be flexible To make new friends, you must have an open and flexible mind. Make sure you are willing to try new things and open to meeting people from every walk of life. This can help expand your perspective and gain knowledge from the experiences of others. This can result in new connections and new opportunities.

Kindness: Treating people with respect and kindness is among the most efficient methods to create lasting and solid friendships. Make sure you are available for your loved ones whenever they require you be there for them, demonstrate empathy and understanding as well as always listening.

While making friends is certainly one of the most crucial aspects of life but having genuine friends is much more essential. There are many ways to meet friends, such as at your social and school activities, but genuine friendships are difficult to find.

What makes a good friend?

A good friend will always be available for you regardless of what. They are there to support you, listen to you and inspire to become the most effective version of you.

True friends make you feel confident about yourself and adds positivity to your day.

They won't criticize you or discuss them behind their backs. They'll keep your secret and will listen whenever you're required to discuss things. True friends will open up to you regardless of whether you find it difficult to accept. They'll tell you the truth since they love you and would like to do what's the best for you.

True friends will be there to help you through the good as well as in bad. They'll celebrate your achievements as well as help your up when you slip. They'll be with all the way through and will never leave you. The truth is that a good friendship partner will always remain by your side, whatever the world throws at you.

There's no need to dress up or act like somebody who you aren't. True friends accept the person you are and is adamantly in love with you. They won't attempt to alter you or change you to someone that you aren't.

Friendships with true value are a rare and valuable gift. It's not every person's dream to find a genuine friend which is fine. However, when you do meet a real partner, you should cherish your relationship and be sure to hold onto them. An authentic friend is always a source of support, love and happiness throughout your day.

What is the best way to become a true FRIEND

A true friendship is about being there to someone in times of need your help, assisting them in both the good and bad times, and creating the ability to stay in touch for a lifetime.

Chapter 6: Conflicting Disagreements About Relationships

It's common for conflicts to occur among you and your buddies. This doesn't mean that you're in bad relations with your friends. Your resolution could make you more close than previously.

Disputs between friends may be difficult, particularly when the emotions are high. It's a crucial element of every relationships. It's good to know there are ways you can aid in making the process easier and more efficient.

Allow each other to breathe If you're feeling angry or frustrated with a person and you're not sure what to say, giving one another an opportunity to breathe can be beneficial. That means taking a moment from chatting or hanging out until you're both able to calm to think about the things you'd like to discuss.

Know when it's time to step off: It's crucial to recognize when disagreement is getting heated and you should walk out before things get worse. It doesn't mean reneging your friendship, but instead having an unintentional break to calm down.

Discuss the issue Once you're at ease to talk, get together with a partner and engage in an honest and honest discussion. You can share your viewpoint regarding what's bothering your as well as take note of what they have to say when they respond. Take a softer and more understanding approach be careful not to attack or accusing the person you are blaming.

Utilize "I" statements: When you want to express your emotions, use "I" statements instead of "you" statements. As an example, instead using the phrase, "You always do this," use the phrase, "I feel upset when this happens." This can help make conversations less threatening and productive.

Don't spread gossip. Avoid saying negative things about a friend. It will only cause more harm and could damage your reputation.

What to do when you need to say sorry: When circumstances are out of control and you've done or said an act that hurts someone, you need to acknowledge the error. An honest apology will go an enormous way to restoring the relationship. Make sure to apologize and acknowledge that you've done wrong and then express your determination to put the right thing happen.

Surround yourself with positivity

It can be difficult at times however, having positive friends can be the most beneficial thing. In those tough times you should be with those who are supportive and love you.

Friendship with positive people will allow you remain optimistic and be focused on the positive things that happen in your life. They'll encourage you to remain your highest, the most optimistic version of yourself. What can you do to find those who can help you to remain positive in your daily life?

Find friends with your beliefs. People who share similar values as well as goals and values tend to be more supportive and appreciate your values. If you are a person who values integrity, kindness and respect, then look for people who share these characteristics.

Friends who are positive are more likely to notice the positive in other people and inspire others to follow suit. Find friends who inspire, are positive and who have a positive approach. The people who push you to become the most effective version of yourself could be extremely valuable. Look for friends who will encourage you to explore new ideas as well as take chances and believe of your capabilities.

If a person causes you to feel negative in your own self-esteem, you need to think about reevaluating the relationship. But, on the other hand when someone constantly encourages you, helps you and helps you feel happy be sure to hold onto your relationship!

Understanding OTHERS A PERSPECTIVE

The ability to understand the viewpoints of others is an important quality of life that helps in building stronger bonds with your fellow citizens. It also helps to make better decisions and look at the world from a different view.

It is ideal to imagine yourself as they do to comprehend another's point of view. Consider what it's like think in their perspective and then try to get a better understanding of their thoughts and opinions. It doesn't mean you must be in agreement with them However, it's important to remember that you're trying to view things through their eyes.

The first step is to pay attention to what people say. If someone is talking to you, give the person your complete attention and attempt to comprehend the meaning behind what they're saying. Be sure not to interrupt them and instead, ask questions that help them clarify their thinking. As an example, you can ask "Can you tell me more about that?" as well as "What made you feel that way?"

Another crucial element of being able to see the other's perspective is empathy. Empathy is the capacity to sense what another experiences, even when you've not experienced the same scenario. For practicing empathy, think about the way you feel similar to the other person in the situation, and attempt to figure out the feelings of another person. This will allow you to reach out to the person on a deeper degree and create a stronger relationship.

Also, it is important to realize that each person has their own lives and experiences, that can influence their outlook. A person that grew up in another culture or has different beliefs might view things differently from you. Be open and consider the views of people around you, even when you don't agree with their views.

In order to fully comprehend others' views, it is important to know your prejudices and preconceptions. Everyone has biases and opinions that influence our perception of the world. These biases could hinder our ability to see the world from a different perspective. To combat this, think about questioning your beliefs and open to new ideas.

In the end, you should be honest and open in conversations with your fellow colleagues. In discussions or debates take the time to discuss or debate in a manner that is cooperative and respect. Be open to the views of others and then share yours respectfully and in a non-judgmental manner. It will aid in building more trusting relationships.

Why are friends occasionally mean because of various factors. It's crucial to realize that people who can be mean to one are usually not trying to hurt each other. Perhaps they're having a hard moment, or be overwhelmed or anxious.

If you're a victim of a friend who's being cruel to you, it's essential to determine what they're saying and talk to them on what their behavior or words can affect your life.

The most prevalent reasons are poor communication and lack of self-esteem. Let's look at these issues one at a.

The term "miscommunication" refers to the misinterpretation of the intentions of each other's words or even actions. One example is that a person may make a joke which could hurt another friend's feelings but not intending to. A friend could arrive late to a scheduled meeting however, the friend thinks they aren't concerned about the event, which can lead to a rift. If this occurs, misunderstandings may lead to arguments which cause tension in the relationship.

Self-esteem issues can cause friendships to be a bit tense with one another. Someone with low self-esteem might feel unsecure and uncertain about them, causing their behavior to be negative towards the other. In particular, they may ridicule the other friends or criticize their behaviour. This could be a defence strategy, since a friend with low self-esteem may think that they feel better in themselves by making others feel down.

Chapter 7: Finding The Perfect First Home

"Okay then I decides to pick the cutest place to live and I apply for it. Then I receive it?

joke- true story. While searching for my first house as an adult of 20 years old I didn't know of the cost of living rentals, lease contracts, credit score or the financial value of having a roommate.

The experience I had was live-it and take-away for me. While I went through the steps along with the sales representative and my mother and I was told that I was a victim of "no credit" and not enough cash for me to "get" any apartment I would like. My mom was required to co-sign my lease. I also had to keep every penny I earned during the season to pay for rent, food as well as books. What a stark reality check!

How can you select the ideal home and what is the best way to pay for it? What are the best ways to find your ideal roommate and what do you do to take on household chores together?

COST OF LIVING

In this day and age, where you're probably still in a school with no income from side hustles or the pocket cash of your parents, finding a home isn't easy. It must be something you like and it should be secure and serene as well as in a position to finance the cost. The amount needed to purchase a safe and comfy home differs across countries as well as the city from city. The living expenses will comprise the expenses of your accommodation, meals, travel clothing, books as well as entertainment and socializing which should be well researched prior to when you begin budgeting although additional expenses will be added in.

For students going to university staying in the same campus may be a good option as well as cost-effective. If staying within the grounds of a private institution can be expensive an amount, living on the private college could be done into a much lower cost. Make selections about which college that you would like to attend and the location of it in accordance with your budget. In addition to these prices, it is also important be prepared for 6-9% to 9-9 percent increase in expenses in the event of an unexpected circumstance or inflation. You should have an additional reserve for costs including furniture, television appliances and insurance on health (if you are not covered by the parent's) and weekend getaways or travel costs to get to home, etc. Don't make the error of not keeping money in reserve for rainy days. This is known as "rainy day funds".

The process of forming a strategy with your caregivers or parents regarding how you can afford the expenses of living when you leave home is among the most important discussions that you'll have as you get older.

It is important to stay in the same boat regarding what you will pay for and the cost of living, so that there is no conflicts and confusion between you.

GIVE SOME CREDIT TO CREDIT SCORES

In order to improve your capacity to control your debt in the future improving your credit score is crucial from the beginning. Credit scores are a numerical representation of your creditworthiness and reliability with regard to finances. The score is utilised by money lending organizations to assess the probability that an person will repay the loan, based on the past history of their. This determines the likelihood that you will receive financial assistance from a financial or banking organization. A high credit score can help you get a lot of money for those who want to rent an apartment or home or purchase a car house, home, or other costly items. You can also get a personal loan or loan, to help you start or grow your business. Similar to the grades you receive, credit scores could be easily lowered however it can be incredibly difficult to increase and that's why it is crucial to understand this in your teens!

The credit score could vary from 300-850. All people start with the credit score at 300. The higher this number higher, the more reliable and accountable you appear to money lending units. Credit scores that are good build your credibility and allows you to obtain better loan terms along with a smoother and faster procedure of approving. Over the long term an excellent credit score is capable to save you hundreds or millions of dollars as you look back, bringing lower interest rates on mortgages for homes or business, vehicles and anything else that requires funding.

Did you notice that the teacher is ignoring minor flaws of students who do well on every examination and achieve a great grade at the conclusion of the academic year? The same manner for students who score high in credit. When you're a creditor with an improved credit score, you'll be considered to have low risk. So, more banks be willing to compete for you with better rates, greater amounts as well as better terms and perks. However, those who do not have a good credit score are viewed as higher of risk, but are not so much favored by banks. An unsatisfactory credit score could negatively impact your odds to get a bargain for renting a home, automobile, or getting life insurance because it impacts your insurance rating. Therefore, overall having a strong financial foundation and being independent and ensuring that the banks will be there for you when you're in trouble can allow you to go into the unknown with confidence.

Here are some tips to boost your credit score. You can do your credit score like a professional

If you do not already have a credit card it is best to make an application for one immediately. It is possible to start by using it to cover your daily needs like gas for your vehicle, etc. You must make sure you pay off the remaining balance on your credit card each month. In time you will build up a credit score that is good and increase the limits and work towards it.

Be sure to check that you pay your bills on time. Payments on time are the primary aspect in improving the credit rating of your. One way to make sure that it is happening are: creating an electronic or physical file that will record all payments as well as unpaid balances and keeping track of a certain day at the beginning of each month to determine whether you've paid the bill the bill, establishing reminders for paying the bills by a set time each month, and paying regular bills to your account at the bank.

Make use of your credit card to pay each payment, and then make sure to pay your credit card in one transaction to avoid ignoring the bill or not paying it. In addition, making use of your credit card on a regular basis can not only boost your score but will also aid you cut costs for a variety of other purchases at the gas pump restaurant, movie theaters and more.

Be diligent in reviewing your credit report regularly. Take out your credit report that you have received from Equifax, Experian, Transunion and other if you reside located in the USA or any other site that applies to your location. After you've obtained the reports, go through them and be aware of where you stand and the areas you need to make improvements. If you have a track record of high account balance on your credit cards and timely payment for credit cards, well-maintained loans and credit cards with a smaller amount of new inquiries credit, you'll score better. Contact your bank to verify if they offer no-cost information about your credit score, and how often they check it.

Try to limit the use of credit up to 30% of available credit, or lower than this. It means that you have to make a decision to pay off your entire credit each month, and if this seems too hard, pay 70% or more of the total credit balance or more, and then try to slowly reduce it to 10 percent. Another way to reduce your credit balance less than 30% is to apply to increase your the credit limit, and to make sure it is higher than what you require so that the proportion of credit utilized always appears smaller in the end.

Be sure to limit your requests for credit cards if you need to apply for too many at a single period of time. If you are applying for loans to purchase a home, a automobile, or a company and a business at the same at the same time, it could appear at times suspicious to banks. They could be doubtful the fact that you're going through an economic crisis within larger perspective and it may affect the credit score of yours.

Create a folder to keep all documents related to credit and enable you to quickly go through your documents whenever needed. If you're an individual who enjoys documents and love the sensation of flipping pages, a physical file is a good option. There is the possibility that it could be lost or misplaced and therefore must be stored and copied in other files, and preferably in a separate location. If you prefer to save the information you want to keep in a soft format, it has the possibility of a computer crash or accidental deletion of the files, which implies the files must also be saved, copied and stored on other devices or drives. The fact is that saving your information into an archive file is a great practice

Consolidate all debts and pay off old debts. If there are accounts from the past that you're paying on, it would make sense to keep the accounts, and pay to them in a gradual manner instead of shutting them down overnight, especially in case improving your score on credit is you are most concerned. If you have missed several installments in your account, pay your debts off or reach a deal with the creditors.

Make use of an application for credit monitoring, and keep track of your progress on a regular basis. The app will tell you whether you require a credit increase for your home purchase. This will help you defend yourself from identity theft as well as fraudulent actions.

Making yourself aware of these tiny factors and taking simple steps will allow you to enhance your credit score in the short-term and in the long run for building a solid financial reputation. It is important increasing your credit score so that you can get a loan for the property or lease it. Find out your credit score and see which homes you could find!

WHAT TO LOOK FOR IN YOUR NEW "PAD"

Finding your first place to live in can be just as exciting as it is terrifying for those who are first-timers. If you're better organized and prepared than I was, searching to find a suitable space is an exhausting process of searching as well as applying for and estimating. Below is a checklist of aspects to think about while assessing every living space:

Determine the budget you have set and ensure that you look for properties that advertise prices that are lower than your budget. Be aware that as you move through the process you'll spend higher in the end. When you first begin your search having a smaller budget that you are able to manage but you'll achieve the amount once things start rolling.

Pick your neighbourhood carefully consider factors such as the proximity to restaurants and work as well as your preference for staying near the bustle of life or return home to peace or quiet, whether you'll take the public transportation system for commutes or you drive your own car, etc. Conduct a thorough study about the neighborhood and make sure you are in security at all times during the day, especially as an young adult, as you don't be able to count on your parents to take care of you!

If you have yourself or intend to purchase one soon be sure to search for parking spaces either in close proximity to or in front of the property or your apartment.

If you are a first-time renter the most important thing aside from being safe and secure of the area is the availability of facilities such as pools, fitness facilities along with laundry facilities that are on-site, as well as other essential needs. You should make a list of all facilities that are essential for you in order to evaluate prospective houses.

You can choose to live on the lower floor in order to minimize the amount of time it takes to get from the home, but still have a decent view, unless you're fortunate enough to have an area of garden OR stay on the top floors, which have less water pressure, which is a result of showers however, they usually have the best views from your home.

Start searching for a place with a bit of space in mind to ensure that you don't have to jump into something in a hurry. Additionally, take care to be open to how quickly or later you are able to move. There are times when your preferred places may be taken up by demand, and you might need to make an application for a while in advance.

Ask as many inquiries you like while your time permits instead of pounding your head against new wall once you've accepted the lease and relocated. Talk to the property owner or broker for an idea of what the procedure for parking is and the facilities that are provided to you, if you are required to pay for bills for utility services and if there are other hidden costs for other than the rental stated in the lease. It is essential to be clear.

Other costs that you must consider in moving is hiring packers and movers, leasing a truck for moving and a renter's insurance buying furniture, and various other household goods. Be aware of expenses which come knocking at your door unexpectedly, such as repair costs as well as cleaning costs once every once in a while.

It is important to read the agreement thoroughly and be sure to understand each point of it prior to signing to the contract. Look for things like the duration of your lease as well as the amount of rent per month as well as the security deposit as well as pet policies, charges for utilities, rules regarding sound, etc.

When you are moving in, be sure to change your address on your mailer and have your home thoroughly and cleaned, if not already done cleaned by the owner. The goal is to have an impression with a clean and fresh start so you're happy getting started!

ALL YOU NEED TO KNOW ABOUT SIGNING THE LEASE

You are probably aware of this, however I'll be asking. Why? It's because it's my responsibility! What is an agreement to lease? It's nothing more than an agreement in writing between a property owner as well as the tenant wishing to lease their property. It defines the fundamental requirements and terms that govern renting the house against cash. The owner is not the only person who signs it the representative, someone like an employee or a family member can sign the agreement if they are legally allowed to make the signing.

In some cases, a written lease agreement can be legally valid and can bind the contract for one year. However, I recommend signing the proper documented and signed agreement in order for clarity in the event that circumstances go wrong. The lease signing process is possible physically and electronically using electronic signatures. Another method of completing the process online is to send the contract to another person, receiving an image of it, then sign it and scanning the agreement to send the document back. Make sure you get the original document you as well since everyone who sign the agreement has the right to get the document.

If you're using an individual cosigner for rent the property, make sure that he or the cosigner is in attendance at the signing. If rent has not been paid or the property is with a mess, it'll put the cosigner on the financial hook, so it's crucial that they attend to the moment that all of the fine print has been taken down and acknowledged.

SHARING WITH A ROOMMATE

The decision of deciding to remain within the same house with someone else is not the same as staying with them for a couple of days, having a cup of coffee or for a night of dancing. Bonding happens when two people are able to get along but so too is the conflict in the event that things do not go as planned. Imagine a situation where you are fighting with someone, or even worse having a conflict, or sharing the sofa to watch a movie in the evening or seeing their smile after a long day, all the time! The search for the ideal roommate is just as crucial as finding that perfect relationship person to share your life with.

Try inviting possible guests to share a room with your family and enjoy time to see how you enjoy and get along. Talk about diverse perspectives of life, and determine how well you are in sync. Discuss bedtimes and time of wake. If you're going to be hosting guests later into the night, and you want your roommate's home to be quiet at 9:15 p.m. If you're a runner, you realize that the likelihood that you will exercise is virtually nonexistent. If you own an animal, verify whether or not he/she likes pets. If you are having a problem with animals, be certain to let it be known before making a commitment to someone who has pets. Many people sleep with clean sheets and an orderly home, while some are not averse to keeping their shoes in the house at all times and treating the living area as a place for the public, rather than cleaning the floors every time. Also, make sure you discuss finances with every prospective roommate to make expectations about the amount of money they will be paying are clear. Do not wish to be stuck with an unpopular roommate, and have to cover everything on your own!

After you've found an appropriate partner and been living together, you should share the responsibilities equally you can and identify each by a name to ensure nobody leaves work without waiting on the other person to finish it. Take care of the people who lives in the house with you and check their thoughts without censoring them. In the case, for example, if they're noise is annoying you or you think your music is bothering them, you can switch on earphones when needed, instead of having a heated debate over which one is the most appropriate way to go. Although spending time or doing activities together can be an excellent way to build an open and friendly relationship but it's important to be aware of when to allow the other person some space. If your roommate's girlfriend or a date has come to visit you It is appropriate to go back to your bedroom. If they're interested They will request for you to stay. It is possible to decline at first time, to make sure that they truly want to. If they really want you then they'll come back to you.

In the case of two grown-ups living in the same residence generally, and open and respectful communication is essential. Communicate with each other in a respectful manner and with openness. If you have to request something from your roommate be sure to do it with calmness and if you are the need to respond, do so respectfully. If you're both capable of doing this and you are able to do this, you'll be prepared not just for the duration of time you share and for the rest of your lives generally.

Chapter 8: What Should I Bring?

"It is only when you leave a home that you know what it was made of!"

UNKNOWN

"A

OK, I got it!

I'm moving to my first home. I'm carrying an Audrey Hepburn poster, my gorgeous pink sheets with polka-dotted patterns, as well as an optimistic outlook on how I will manage my own apartment for the very first time!"

That was my thought when I walked through the front door into my home. Clean beige carpet as well as bright white walls it was a new beginning for me to be independent at first. When I began setting up my images and taking my clothes off I discovered that I had a lot of items I did not think I'd require. I had dishes but no dish soap. I was able to wash my clothes but there was no laundry basket. There was a spotless carpet however I would have to clean it in the near future. Every discovery led me back to the department store several times it, back and forth between months, before I got all the small items I required to be able to live. It was a lot more going to the shop than the items I required. Did you know that a house requires such a large amount of money?

In this section we will walk through all the small things that we'll need around the home and the things we do not. Where can you purchase those basic items in your area in order to avoid spending more in time and cash on traveling? What are the best places to shop for essentials for your home on the budget? What are the basics that we're discussing? There are many issues which arise when you begin your new adventure under the shelter. Do you think about knowing all of them ahead of time and enjoying the journey of moving out instead of stressing about it? Let's move!

SOME CHECKLISTS FOR "THE BIG MOVE"

While you fill the blank space of your home, take a look at every room using checklists to help you remember the essentials you need to be able to. While you're there, don't neglect to decorate each space by putting your own stamp on it by adding photos, artwork rug, prints as well as other items. Incorporating your roommates in the planning process is an excellent idea to ensure you are able to share costs and reduce the number of redundancies.

Be aware that if you're in a tight spot, like many people of your age do, you shouldn't be afraid of buying second-hand furniture, such as an old washer, used refrigerator or anything else which can help you save money. It is not necessary to feel embarrassed when you go into the thrift store or the internet for the items that you desire. It's very normal among young people to shop for cheap, utilized items. And it can be beneficial for the planet!

Kitchen

If you intend to cook at the home frequently ensure that your kitchen is stocked with all the necessary equipment.

Cooking Essentials

3 Frying pans: small medium, and large

3 saucepans- small, medium, large

Basic cooking tools- the spatula and large spoon spoon with slotted

Other cooking tools - Tongs and whisks or pasta spoon

Colander

3 mixing bowls: small medium, and large

2 cookie sheets

Broiler pan

8x8 in. glass baking dish

9x12 in. glass baking dish

Kitchen scissors

Measuring cup set

Measurement spoon set

Cutting board

Chopping knife

Useful Kitchen Gadgets

Can Opener

Meat thermometer for meat

Basting Brush or Baster

Pizza Cutter

Cheese Grater

Basic Appliances

Coffee Maker/ Tea Kettle

Hand Mixer

Toaster oven or toaster

Blender

Rice cooker

Required Dishes - The quantity of each is contingent on the number of roommates you share

Small plate, larger plates cups, bowls

Drinking glasses

A set of butter knives, forks as well as spoons

Steak knives

Glass storage containers that have lids- small medium, large

Other Important Items

Plastic Wrap

Aluminum Foil

Parchment paper

Plastic Baggies- sandwich, pint, gallon

Kitchen towels

Reusable napkins

Paper towels

Oven Mitts

The trash can and the trash bags

Chefs with more experience or baker.

Tins of muffins

Racks for cooling

Pizza pan

Bread pan

Rolling pin

Living Room

To create a social hub in the house, you should focus on relaxation and enjoyment.

Furniture

Couch (if you decide to purchase an old couch that's not visually appealing, you can use the couch cover to make it appear like new!)

Coffee Table

Chairs for sitting

Lamps

A cabinet or shelf to store books, board games photographs, and other items.

Entertainment

Television

Video game console

Board games

Bluetooth Speaker

Useful Accessories

Throw pillows

Put blankets on

Rug

Coasters

Dining Area

It is usually a small area in your home, it might be beneficial to keep dining areas basic, and with personal elements like centerpieces to provide a relaxing dining space.

Chairs and dining table

Centerpiece

Placemats and tablecloths, if needed

Bedroom

It will be your personal space where you'll be spending the majority of your time. Utilize your creativity to build your own space that's not just practical, but also shows your character and keeps you satisfied.

Furniture

Bed frame or platform bed

Mattress

5 - or 6-drawer dresser

Night time stand

Lamp

Desk

Shelves

TV

Trashcan

Comfy Cozy

Sheets

Pillows

Comforter/ Duvet, and cover

Extra sheets

Area rug

Extra blanket for cold nights

Closet items

Shelf or shoe rack

Full Length Mirror

Clean clothing Hamper

Hangers

Coat Hangers

Bathroom

Although not the most beautiful space in the house however, it's an vital one. What is important here is organization and hygiene so that you and your roommate be in this space together however, other people using bathrooms will not be frightened at the smell and sight.

Essentials

Liner and shower curtain

Shower rings for curtain

Trash can

Holder for the toothbrush

Hand soap dispenser

Towelsfor shower facial, washcloths, and towel

Bath rug washable

Towel bath mat

Toilet paper

Holder for toilet paper (if the landlord does not provide it)

These checklists can be used as a starting point and incorporate items you believe are necessary to be included. The only thing I would suggest is to establish a reasonable budget and then try to incorporate things in the budget. Learn about your personal habits to understand the priorities you have. In the case of example, if have a limited budget perhaps you should start by buying an un-floored mattress and then save to buy an actual mattress. For instance, if you're an avid griller purchase a grill that you can cook outdoors and save money on baking sheets and cookware. The idea is obvious.

Making it on your own the first time may be somewhat nerve-wracking, but by planning a bit and a well-planned approach and you'll be able for your next challenge in confidence!

KEEPING IT CLEAN

"Once you learn how to see how your inner turmoil manifests itself through your surroundings, you can reverse engineer this, mastering yourself by mastering the space in which you live."

SHOUKEI MATSUMOTO I was a Type A person. I was a perfectionist, and kept my home well-organized and clean. My dirty roommate was an incredibly scary experience for me. Her laundry pile could often reach the ceiling. If she could do all her laundry in one day, she could take the stack to the mountains on a weekends. Her usual routine was to purchase new clothes, and then start wearing them and turn off those clothes that required to be washed. A few days ago I realised that her cups were disappearing from the kitchen. As I walked into her bedroom, I discovered several cups stuffed with water, milk that had been spoiled and fermented juice. I would like to put on an hazmat suit prior to entering the room. The days of uncleanliness are over but the stench and dust from her unkept environment don't seem to disappear from my thoughts. If you are living in a filthy home and you create an unhealthy environment for yourself, but you also create an object of ridicule to those in the vicinity. Do not wish to be someone who is so filthy that your partner is so afflicted that she has to write about it in her book many years afterwards! It is better to discuss the dirt than simply sweeping it away under the rug.

Chapter 9: Cleaning Supplies

Before starting be sure to are stocked with the supplies you require. Begin to gather these items prior to moving into. Do not wait until you have insects swarming the kitchen, or there is an unattractive black ring on the toilet before you can get the cleaning products you need.

These constitute the absolute minimum needed to keep your house clean:

Toilet Scrubber brush

Cleansing toilet bowls

Sanitizing wipes

Plunger

Rubber gloves

Nonabrasive tub and shower cleaner

Cleaning Wipes, or cleaning products

Baby wipes

Sponges

Scrubbing sponges

Clean pumice stone

Bucket

Mop

Vacuum

Broom and dust collection

Cleaning Cloths, also known as "dirt rags" or "dust cloths"

Paper towels

Glass cleaner

All-purpose cleaner

White Vinegar

Carpet stain cleaner for those who are carpeted

TIPS TO CLEAN YOUR OWN HOUSE

The germs are everywhere in the house, and they can get in areas that you aren't. Some common areas where germs remain but aren't able to cleanse include your keyboard on the computer and your cutting board in the kitchen, cash the main sofa in which you relax and watch television and soccer, your fitness tracker for everyday use bag or purse and your remote for the TV as well as your mobile phone, which is likely to be communicating with your more than any other device in the world.

You can certainly do your own cleaning and we'll talk on later in the discussion of the best cleaning plan However, for most people it is not the need for the "cleaning day." You can spend an hour doing a thorough clean-up of your home so you don't have to do as much chores in the midst of an active daily life. There are two options for performing the "cleaning day." One is by room, and the otherin the form of chores. You decide the method that you find most appealing. If you are a housekeeper, then either you complete all the tasks in every space as you travel around the house and you take care of all of the dusting, followed by all the vacuuming the house, and then vacuuming up. We'll learn some quick techniques for this kind of clean-up.

Store all the cleaning tools in a bucket or caddy and use it as a the storage you can take with you when moving between rooms. In this way, you'll be prepared for your clean-up journey. You will not need to think about the place your tools are once you've started.

The baby wipes can be a less expensive alternative to cleansers and they are simple to carry throughout the home when it is necessary to wipe items down. They are not disinfecting, however they can be used to clean wooden floors, cabinetry, staircases, etc.

It is recommended to clean from the top down to ensure that dust at the top is deposited on the floor, and it then is cleaned.

Prior to beginning the task of cleaning you should take a walk through the home and clean things that are clogging your home, from old clothes to magazines which have to get rid of. Put them away in a location where you can clearly see which items go into the trash and the rest are able to be given away. Also, if an item isn't given any place to call home, it must have one or has to be removed.

Strip your beds, and wash the sheets, as well as couch blankets, while you do the remainder of your chores.

Dusting:

1. Shut off your ceiling fan prior to beginning your dusting. While you're doing your cleaning, you should do this prior to cleaning your room also, to ensure the dust

that has accumulated gets cleaned out during the cleaning process.

2. Make sure you dust the furniture's tops on the tops of your shelves, beneath the shelves along the handrails and behind picture frames TV screens, and any other small knick-knacks. Utilize a bent, long mop to scrub places that are difficult for a mop to reach such as higher shelves or blinds. If you don't own one, you can tie one of the microfiber cloths at the top of the bristle and put it on the.

3. Make use of a microfiber towel or glass cleaner to wash every mirror and glass item as well as surfaces all in one step.

4. Additionally, you can clean the all hard surfaces in the home including countertops, cabinets doors, knobs, remotes and phones at the same time.

5. Make sure to clean bathrooms fans as well as air vents and air intakes, where dust accumulates for better air quality.

Vacuuming

1. Clean out the canister prior to cleaning the filters with a vacuum each couple of months

2. Make use of carpet and hard flooring settings to wash the correct floor.

3. Make use of your vacuum cleaner to wash the baseboards, furniture and the stairs, if you have them.

Bathroom:

1. Shower and tub: Apply the tile cleaner or gentle cleanser such as Bon Ami to spray or sprinkle over the surfaces. It will break down the dirt and stain after which you can give the surface a rub, and scrub the area. Make use of a sponge scrubber to clean the area. Wash with hot water making use of a cup or hand-held shower pipe. If you own a cloth shower curtain, rinse it with the washing machine. If you've got a vinyl curtain, clean it using the sponge.

2. Toilet Cleansing: Use a toilet cleaner as well as a toilet brush to cleanse the inside of the toilet. Turn the toilet brush up so that you can access the top of the bowl. This is the place the place where the majority of the grossness occurs. Make sure you push the toilet brush down into the toilet's hole in the lower part of the toilet. Then provide it with a thorough scrub. Utilize a disinfectant cleaner clean under the seat of the toilet and on the over the seat of the toilet as well as the flusher and the upper part of the toilet. If you spot an unnatural water ring inside the toilet that you aren't able to remove using a brush, you can use a pumice rock to clean the ring off.

3. Every few months Clean the bowl of water at the back of the toilet. Lift the lid on the water tank, and add 3-4 cups of vinegar. After it's spent about an hour in the tank shut off the water source and drain the water. This can help to drain the tank, and after that you can wash it off.

4. Floor: Apply a disinfectant cleaner, or a homemade mixture consisting of alcohol, vinegar, and essential oils to clean the floor of your bathroom. If you own rugs you can wash them using the dryer or washer.

5. Sink Cleaning: Use all-purpose cleaner, or the similar disinfectant cleaners to scrub the bowl of your sink and then wipe the counter.

Kitchen:

1. Make sure you clean the outside and inside of microwaves and refrigerators.

2. Take care to clean small appliances, such as your coffee maker, toaster as well as everything else you can find in the kitchen counter.

3. Clear the counters, stovetop and the sides of any large appliance

4. Clean up with disinfectants the exterior and interior of your trash can

5. Once you have finished the food After you have finished eating, apply a gentle cleaner such as Bon Ami and soap such as Dawn as well as a green sponge to scrub the kitchen sink. Cleanse the sink with hot water.

6. Remove dust from the cabinets' front

7. Cleanse the interior of your microwave by heating some vinegar in a dish in the microwave, to melt the residue and then wipe it off with a microfiber wipe.

8. Clean or sweep floors and then clean with mop or wiping.

9. If your dishwasher is on clean the top of the door's interior and also the place underneath the rubber flap that is at the point where the bottom door is closed. The areas that collect dirt and mold and need to be cleaned frequently.

10. Each month you'll need to wash your oven, to keep away from the risk of fires

from grease, and also to ensure that the food you cook in good taste. In order to clean your oven begin by cleaning using a sponge along with some good soap for fighting grease. If you have difficult to clean places, make use of the pumice stones and soap and scrub. Clean the soap with hot water and an absorbent sponge. Next, soak your oven racks in the sink overnight in hot vinegar and water. After waking, scrub them down using a sponge. And voilà! an oven that is clean!

If you share an roommate plan a day of cleaning together and share chores.

YOU'RE CLEANING SCHEDULE

Based on the dimensions of your home, the consumption, the number of guests staying in the home as well as the types of flooring and furniture to choose from, you can develop an outline of the things you need to do daily, weekly, each month, and every year. In order to make cleaning more easy make sure you are comfortable in keeping clutter at a minimum. make sure your bathrooms are dry and clean Clean up spills and crumbs quickly when they happen make sure you wash your hands regularly and dry shoes on the way to the entrance or get rid of shoes prior to going into your house to prevent dust and dirt coming into your home from the outside. The typical clean-up routine will look something as follows:

Daily: Clean the kitchen counters and kitchen tables. Clear the kitchen, throwing food waste away. Clean the kitchen's floor as well as under the tables. Get rid of clutter in the home including junk mail, newspapers or dirty clothes, grocery items not being used, and everything else lying around on the floor in an unsuitable spot.

Every week, scrub the bathroom sink, kitchen sink and the toilet. Get rid of old food items out of your refrigerator and scrub the fridge before adding new food items. Vacuum floors. Change the towels in the kitchen and bathroom.

Monthly Showers and tubs that are clean. Wash bed sheets as well as house blankets. Wipe mirrors, floors and windows. Clean air duct inlets and exhausts. Refresh the kitchen sponge.

QUALITY: Clear out the cupboards and pantry. Clean the oven and then filter the dishwasher. Use a clean wash cycle using bleach in the clothes washer. Plan an "cleaning day" to wipe off and scrub everything around your home.

Every year: Clean your curtains by washing them or wiping them clean with a the help of a sponge. Take a look through your closet as well as personal items and donate unneeded items. Get windows cleaned, clean carpets, and clean the surfaces of cabinets as well as the refrigerator's top. The oven and refrigerator should be moved towards the front to clean under the surface.

It is possible that you will need to perform one or more of these tasks frequently based on a couple of factors, for instance the presence of pets, or if you suffer from a serious dust allergy or live in an area that is dusty, or where there's construction.

If you're feeling indulgent and fancy, then you could call a local company and have a thorough cleaning of your house at the conclusion of the year, prior to the holidays, although this can be performed every 3 years, too.

If you manage to maintain a steady pace with the chores listed above, you'll not only be able to enjoy a lovely home that smells and is comfortable as well, you'll have fewer insects to contend with, and will probably get sicker. If you host guests in your home, they'll be comfortable and feel welcome with a clean and tidy your home.

A third important task to clean is doing laundry.

LAUNDRY DAY

"Cleaning and organizing is a practice, not a project."

MEAGAN FRANCIS

ONe It was a summer night, and I was preparing for a big party. I had a great time taking some time to prepare, just like often...

I went through my closet, and pulled out the gorgeous green skirt I in mind to wear with my brand new white shirt, and gold hoops. It is said that you should be yourself which was exactly my idea to walk in at the event with the new friends I made who I worked with during my summer job. It was planned to have dinner in a posh French eatery in downtown. As I took the skirt back on the way, I noticed it was wrinkled after being hung on the clothesline. I quickly went to the laundry room and started pressing it onto the iron table. This, happens to be an essential part of the checklist of appliances that are small in the family. My surprise was when the iron caught on my skirt about halfway. It would not move. I pulled it out using a lot of force and saw one black mark in the form of iron on the skirt. I panicked, and then jumped. I've seen my mom ironing clothes effortlessly. What was wrong? After that, I discovered that it is important to know how to clean my clothes. Did you think it was an learned ability?

I made a mess of a few of my clothes due to inexperience, but it's not necessary to. The laundry process initially appears to be an unending stream of laundry that require continual pampering and care. Don't stress. There's a lot to do in the present, but with the help of a few tools at home, you'll get used to the art of taking care of your little ones quickly enough. Also, make sure to wash the appliances that keep your clothes dry in the course of time. It will help them function more efficiently and help keep bad smells away.

There's good news, the majority of clothes have directions about what you need to do, on a tag that's on the product. If you're able to follow instructions that you follow, you're able to wash your clothes! There are a couple of directions that you don't must adhere to. It could mention "wash warm" but you could wash cold, and conserve the warm water. Then, it might advise dry cleaning however a gentle wash, hand wash, and dry air is right to reduce the dry cleaning cost. You can also find instructions on ironing clothing and if I'd had the knowledge I would have gotten the green dress. Since then, I've learned to use the steamer over an iron. Steamers are easy on clothes and is perfect for delicate fabrics such as silk, chiffon, or some polyester. Use the iron only for clothing items like trousers and suits or jeans as well as the khaki trousers.

If you're in a position to choose then it's best to install a sink in your laundry area where you could wash your clothes by hand, and apply specific treatments to areas of the garment that are stained. Baking soda can be a substitute for chemical agents used to eliminate staining and smells from clothing. It also helps help to brighten and clean your laundry. If you happen to buy baking soda in your kitchen, put it in to wash your washing!

TO DRY-CLEAN OR NOT TO DRY-CLEAN- THAT IS THE QUESTION!

If you purchase clothing, certain labels will read "dry-clean only". These clothes need to dry-clean the garments. Other brands will mention "dry clean". That means that the manufacturer is suggesting you dry clean the clothing, however there's the option of washing it yourself if you have some effective and safe methods.

The fabrics like silk and taffeta as well as acetate, velvet, and wool should be taken to dry cleaning services, but cotton, linen acrylic, nylon, polyester as well as cashmere may be easily cleaned in your home with additional consideration. When you are washing the entire fabric, do a small test to determine whether the color has a tendency to fade enough. Making a cotton swab moist with soft soap and then applying it to a portion of the clothing that is invisible is a great thing to use. If you spot the dye bleeding, then you be able to figure out what you can dogo to a cleaner's.

If you are planning to view the delicate clothes you wear at the comfort of your own home, there's a few points to bear in your mind. If the item which does not scream "dry-clean only" is durable and has passed your blood test then you can wash it by hand with the most gentle setting. A second tip is to take the garment inwards out, and then place it in a bag for washing before washing it with an easy and short cycle. It will lessen the friction and force on the exterior of the fabric or its side which will be exposed. After you have cleaned, lay the clothes on a smooth surface for it to dry.

HAND WASHING LIKE A BOSS

Washing your hands is by far the most basic method to wash your clothes. It's been used for the longest duration. In the case of dry-clean clothing, hand washing is a good option and can save the cost of washing your clothes. This technique has been well-tested and has been tested. It just requires a few supplies including detergent, water an unclean towel, and an ample space such as the bathtub, bucket or sink.

Clean up the area where you'll washing your clothes hand-in-hand. Then fill the bucket or tub with water. Be sure to allow enough headroom for the garment as well as your hands to move. You can add a little detergent, based on the quantity of garments and the amount of water. Then, put the clothes in the solution for detergent, and move into the water. Change the clothes to allow it to absorb the detergent. After the garment has been affected by the detergent, you can utilize your hands to create an action similar to that machines can do to garments. Let the garments soak within this solution. Choose the amount of time to soak according to the softness of the garment as well as the temperature of the water. As an example, cotton is able to be soaked for longer than silk.

Be careful not to overuse detergents in order to be certain you're not forced to print until the hair turns gray. Take the detergent liquid in the tub, then wipe the tub clean of any leftover lather. If you are washing fibers that are strong, it is possible to let the faucet go through them and wash faster, but this won't be appropriate to wash delicate garments.

Take the clothes off of their water and press the garment down to release the final stream of water. The garment should be flattened on the dry towel, then make it roll up. Pressing to release extra water, then laying it onto a dry towel will result in the government dam un-wet. This will basically replicate the drying settings that is used in washing machines in this case, and help to make air drying more quickly.

While it can be time-consuming and time-consuming, washing delicate clothing will prolong the lifespan of their garments and help preserve their colour and form. If you're moving to a house without washer or dryer, washing hand certain clothes could save you money on the laundry mat.

Chapter 10: Settings Of Your Washer

The three main functions that are present in each washing machine are duration of the cycle (duration) and the speed at which the cycle is performed and how hot the water is. A lot of modern washers permit you to personalize your washing cycle by altering these independently. Look for one that allows you greater control over the washing process, if it is possible. If you don't buy a flex-based machine it is possible that you will be spending more to dry clean later on.

The duration of the cycle in the timer in the machine will determine how long it can clean the clothes you've loaded it. Clothes that have less dirt and delicate may be cleaned with shorter cycles, while clothes that require extensive and rigorous washing require more time. You should consider choosing the shortest cycle to get what you need done. The shorter cycles mean lower energy consumption, and greater time for washing the clothes. For a successful process I recommend that placing your laundry in separate bags for laundry based on the degree of dirtiness.

The rate of cycle depends on the amount of force it uses as well as the number of spins the blades must go through to spin and spin the clothes within it. You can choose for this to be done with a slow/slow, speed/slow and fast/fast movement. The speed/fast settings for large items as well as towels since they're suited for the process where both the wash cycle as well as the process of training will be swift. The slow/fast or permanent press cycle works for fabric that has an tendency to get wrinkled. This means that the washing process is fast, however the spin is slow. This helps can reduce wrinkles in garments when they are taken from the machine. This is the case for all of your clothes. The third cycle is slower or delicate and is suitable for delicate and gentle fabrics like the name implies, with washing and draining are done at a slow pace.

The temperature of water can also be a crucial element in washing your laundry correctly. Many detergents and equipment nowadays are made to function perfectly using cold water. Utilizing cold water saves energy and therefore saves money as well as being more respectful to the sheets and clothing you wear. The use of hot water is recommended in the case of items with a lot of dirt, like towels or white clothing that aren't at risk loss of the color. The hot water can provide simple cleaning. However, it can leave the fabric with a fade after prolonged usage. If you don't want to spend too much time thinking about it the use of cold water can seem like a no-brainer.

SETTINGS OF YOUR DRYER

Like your hair and clothes, laundry should be dried in the air. However, we don't have the space, time and the patience to afford our clothes that luxurious. Dryers are among the greatest innovations in modern technology, making our lives easier but drying too much can cause a closet of faded, shrinking or sagging clothes in no time.

Regular typically produces the most heat, and is ideal for sweatshirts, jeans Hoodies, towels, and many other garments that are heavy. Although the name implies regular, it is a reference to heavy in all manner.

Permanent Press: heat is at medium, and provides an opportunity to cool down after basic drying process has been completed. This helps in the reduction of wrinkles on the majority of your sheets and laundry.

Delicate is the smallest level of heat. It generally referred to in the form of "low heat". Wearing clothes with elastics, spandex and soft cotton as well as linen, laces, and wool work well in this kind of environment.

The No-Heat and Fluff settings are ideal for delicate garments can also be washed with no heat, and is often referred to with the words "tumble-dry". Clothes with embellishments, sequins embroidery, sequins, or any other decorations must dry in this setting regardless of how long it requires.

WASHING TIPS

Let's quickly look over some tips that can aid in making washing your clothes easier and will keep your clothes in good condition over time.

Make sure to wash your clothes only the amount of times that are is necessary, at cleaning at home or in the salon'. Each every time you wash them you reduce the life span of your clothes slowly. If the shirt you wore at the event last night does not smell dirty, but is somewhat unpleasant, think about placing it in the sun for a few hours to rid it of odor the smell instead of putting it in the washing machine. If you had the undershirt underneath a top, you should give the garment another wash before washing.

Wash at lower temperatures, and with shorter cycle times as you can, and take care when washing your clothes in order to keep the color and fiber healthier over time. The bed linens and undergarments might require exceptions for thorough cleaning since they are in direct contact with bodily fluids and invisible dirt. They could also be the host for germs.

Pay attention to the labels for care on your clothing and follow guidelines for the garment which needs to be cleaned dry and stored.

Do not purchase garments that require to be dry-cleaned only in order to spare your self the hassle of going to dry cleaning service and saving our environment from the negative effects on fibers in textiles.

Make sure you choose environmentally friendly detergents and laundry powders. Consider laundry detergent sheets that can help save the environment by reducing plastic.

Wash your clothing in the inside of the washer to reduce friction between the surfaces of the clothes, and thus harm to fibres.

Dry your clothes by air when you are able to. This is better to protect your clothing and your environment as compared to dryers that tumble dry.

Pick a cool and dry area to safeguard your clothing from moisture or heat as well as sun however, make sure you unlock the doors to the closet, and keep them cooled periodically.

Don't over-fill your closets with clothes, washing machines, and dryers are not good ideas to ensure the longevity of your clothing.

Choose velvet or padded hangers to hang clothing. Make sure to hang your clothes especially prone to wrinkle.

HOW TO TAKE CARE OF YOUR APPLIANCES

Making sure you take care of your appliances that you wash is equally important as caring for your clothes that are put into the appliances.

Check that your dryer is clean to ensure that air can be clean and cleaned. If airways become blocked the moist air can get stuck in the drum along with the clothes. Enhancing the effectiveness of your dryer will speed up drying time and help save energy and cash. If one cycle of drying can be efficient enough, then it will be unnecessary to dry the clothing another time. The lint trap should be cleaned each time you load a load into. Each year, you have to clean your air hose and vents in order to ensure it runs effectively. Make sure to spin your clothes an more time before washing in order to eliminate any water. This will result in less tension on the dryer. Also, make sure to allow some space in the dryer even when it's working. The dryer should be filled to the brim with about two thirds of the space it has is a great idea. The clothes will need room to dry and tumble.

The washer needs to be cleaned at least once every 3 to 6-months at most. For cleaning your washing machine, put some bleach in the cup for bleach, which is usually marked clearly in the washing machine. Many new washers feature an exclusive "clean" cycle. If not, a simple wash is sufficient. Once the cycle has been completed then take a damp cloth and clean the drum, as there are pieces of dirt that didn't disappear. It is possible to use the bristles of your toothbrush to clean any remaining residue from the dispensers compartments. Use a commercial cleaner or mix in some vinegar or baking soda from the pantry. Additionally, you can use a towel with some vinegar and a cloth to clean the bottom of the drum (the rubber part that lies between the door to the washer as well as the drum) and the inside of the lid on top of the lid and the place where you can find the control panel.

As we require our regular maintenance, relaxation, and room, so do appliances.

If you've never had to do laundry before, it's an excellent idea to begin when you get your home. Your parents will supervise you and help you with the task while you training so that once you're alone you'll be ready to start! Once you've mastered the drying and washing requirements of your clothes, washing becomes a regular chore that you manage with ease.

Back to Pizza!

"Life is about sharing. If we're skilled in something, we should pass it to others."

MARY BERRY

Do you remember that, at the very beginning of the book we discussed adulthood as being a pizza with a pepperoni topping? We'll revisit this analogy for a minute... since everyone loves speaking about pizza? !

Remember your last time ordering pizza for your group of group of friends. There are many different ways that this could look however it's always about the same aspect which is sharing. In the event that you're all ordering each pizza with diverse toppings, you will share details. They warn one another if the temperature is still too hot that you're going to cause a tear in your lips off. You also discuss your opinions on the toppings you choose You may also swap one or two slices.

Pizzas were designed to be shared also, as are the contents of information. When the time arrives for the pizza delivery man of adulthood to arrive and you're ready, it's an excellent opportunity for you to discuss the things you've learned with your pals so that they are aware of what to expect when they reach adulthood (and do not get their mouths burned by pizza!)

It's possible to go higher - aid me in spreading information to teenage girls who you've never had the pleasure of meeting! As when you leave an online review about your favourite pizza joint the only thing it takes just a few seconds of your time.

When you write a review about the book through Amazon by leaving a review, you'll be able to inform other children the best place to find needed information to be ready for the adult world.

By letting potential readers learn how this book been helpful to you, and the information they'll discover inside and teach them how to be sure to know what temperature is ideal to get the best value from your pizza. Do I take this pizza metaphor to far? Never!

Thank you for helping me reach many more people. This information is essential not to be shared.

BEING SMART WITH GROCERIES

"Whoever said money can't buy happiness simply didn't know where to go shopping."

GERTRUDE STEIN My mother was a health-conscious. She was very strict about my diet and the contents of my fridge was stocked with that I would hide my noodle packets in my room and cook the noodles only when away. As I left the house for the first time it was among my most thrilling moments for me. I was now able to purchase any food item I needed and have any moment I desired. Naturally, I was smitten. I would walk through the aisles of the store's shelves and begin to grab anything and everything that felt good. Beyond food, I was able to taste freedom. I began to experience. The feeling was amazing over the next 6 months. But then, the reality struck me with a hammer. I lost everything I had and gaining 20lbs in two months! This is when I realised that I needed to learn what to look for in the grocery store in order to have healthier eating habits and not overspend my savings. Here are some tips to keep in mind as you head to the market when you next go there.

There are numerous benefits to eating fruits and vegetables in the summertime. They bring newness and freshness to your meals It is also lighter on your budget, and also adds nutrients to your meals. If you purchase vegetables or fruit that aren't supposed to be local during the time of season It means they were grown from elsewhere and imported. A longer travel time could result in the loss of nutrients along the journey, an increase in carbon footprint and recouping the cost lost on transportation.

One of the most popular myths says that fresh fruit and veggies are healthy for your overall health. Let's break it down. If the fruits and vegetables you buy are packed with flash-frozen and frozen in their peak freshness, then you'll never be deprived of the nutritional benefits that accompany the freshness. These are usually less expensive and more durable because they don't run the risk of spoiling in the shortest time, and also make it easier to visit the supermarket.

Go to the farmers market to help support the local economy and are able to examine the origins of how the food is raised. It also means you can buy products that have been produced earlier than what you can find at the grocery stores.

Make sure to get toward the back of the display to look for more recent produce since sales employees usually are told to store them at the back of the store in order to rotate the products. Be sure to keep an eye out for expiry dates in order for a time-bound finish.

Other than emergencies where you're in a rush to make time for preparing your dinner, not buy fruits or vegetables cut in pre-cut pieces. They can make your pocket more. The skin and assortment of fruit and vegetables are meant to guard the skin and should be removed just before you eat them.

All vegetables and fruits should be cleaned however, only before you eat them. If you wash them after you return after grocery shopping may reduce the life span of your fruits and vegetables.

It is true that a great book can't be evaluated on its appearance. Also, evaluate the quality and value of your fruits or vegetable based on its weight that indicates its amount of water it has as well as its skin, which signifies its health, instead of looking for a well-designed and balanced item of food.

Avoid the grocery store on Saturdays, as everybody else because deliveries typically arrive earlier in the week for the stores that will give you a more fresh foods.

Go to the local nurseries and see if you can grow some fruits and veggies from your garden at home. Get started eating your own natural produce, instead of purchasing every item you see on the market. What's the chance? It could be just the pastime you've been searching for.

Make sure to keep fruits, vegetables as well as eggs, fish or nuts in your top priorities during shopping. You should also limit snacks like cookies and chips to occasions like special events or movie night. Keep in mind that you'll tend to consume more calories from what you keep in your storage.

www.ingramcontent.com/pod-product-compliance
Lightning Source LLC
Chambersburg PA
CBHW071443080526
44587CB00014B/1975